Patrick Gordon Walker

THE CABINET

JONATHAN CAPE

THIRTY BEDFORD SQUARE LONDON

FIRST PUBLISHED APRIL 1970
REPRINTED 1970

© 1970 BY PATRICK GORDON WALKER

JONATHAN CAPE LTD
30 BEDFORD SQUARE, LONDON, WCI

SBN 224 61819 9

PRINTED IN GREAT BRITAIN
BY EBENEZER BAYLIS AND SON LTD
THE TRINITY PRESS, WORCESTER, AND LONDON
BOUND BY JAMES BURN AND CO. LTD, ESHER, SURREY

CONTENTS

Contents

PART THREE   CABINET IN ACTION

PART FOUR   FURTHER QUESTIONS

PREFATORY NOTE

In this book I make allusions to a number of recent events without giving particulars of the persons involved or details of what was decided.

I have prepared a key elucidating these passages which will, I hope, in due and proper course appear in later editions.

I would like to thank a number of people who have been good enough to read and comment on the typescript of this work. I am particularly grateful to Dr Anthony King of Essex University and to Mr David Butler, Fellow of Nuffield College, Oxford, for their most valuable suggestions. I am, of course, myself wholly and exclusively responsible for everything in the text.

Mr Michael Clarke, Lecturer in Politics at the University of Edinburgh, prepared the table of Cabinet Committees that appears on pp. 176 and 177.

In order to avoid cluttering up pages with footnotes, I have gathered these together towards the end of the book in order of chapters.

As I dislike ibids and op. cit.s in a list of notes, I quote only the surname of the author or some similar brief reference to a work. After the notes I append a list containing fuller particulars of books cited in the text.

For Alan and Robin

PART ONE

Political Environment

CHAPTER 1

SURVIVAL OF THE CABINET

(1) Seat of Political Authority

'*The post-war epoch has seen the final transformation of Cabinet Government into Prime Ministerial Government*'[1]—thus Mr Crossman in his brilliant introduction to Bagehot's *English Constitution*, writing in 1963 before he had himself served in a Cabinet.

The year before, Mr John Mackintosh had expressed a similar, though more qualified, view: 'Now the country is governed by the Prime Minister.'[2]

Cabinet Government has been written off before. Bagehot's book appeared in 1867: in the chapter added to the new edition of 1872 he deplored that subsequent changes had denatured the balanced, well-working system he had previously described. In his view the extension of the franchise would make Parliament unworkable because it would produce incompatible and irreconcilable interests.[3] The Cabinet that arose out of Parliament must become equally unworkable.

Lord Campion, then Clerk of the House, writing in 1952, claimed that 1832–68—Bagehot's period—was the golden age of the Cabinet. Since then it had in his view degenerated.[4]

Nowadays the mode is to assert that the British system of government is being assimilated to the American and that in consequence the whole Cabinet structure is being or has been transformed.

Mr Crossman writes that even before 1867 events had given the Prime Minister 'near-Presidential powers'—thus curtailing Lord Campion's golden age: that 'the British Cabinet has now come to resemble the American Cabinet' (which notoriously can be ignored and overridden by the President). Mr Crossman epitomizes his conclusion in

13

a cross-heading to a section of his introduction to Bagehot: 'THE PASSING OF CABINET GOVERNMENT.'[5]

Lord Campion came to a corresponding judgment: a Member of Parliament, 'like a delegate to the electoral college for the election of an American President, is returned primarily as a tied voter for a potential Prime Minister.'[6]

Such implicit or explicit dismissals of Cabinet government seem to me erroneous. They over-dramatize very important changes that have indeed occurred in the role of the Cabinet—and thus get them out of focus and perspective.

The Cabinet of the 1950s and 1960s can be traced back through a line of continuous descent from the eighteenth century. 'The Cabinet was an eighteenth-century solution of the problem that distracted the whole of the seventeenth century.'[7] This problem was how to strike a balance between the Crown and a representative Parliament. In the CivilWar Parliament governed alone and Committees of the House assumed executive functions. This presupposed a nearly unanimous House of Commons: executive bodies cannot accommodate open argument and dispute between organized groups. Dissidents had to be purged or Parliaments nominated. The Restoration brought an uneasy balance between King and Parliament. After the Revolution Parliament tried to counter the King's power by the Place Act which kept his Ministers out of the House; but Parliament could no more than before exercise executive functions and it forfeited the power to influence Ministers. In the eighteenth century 'the executive authority of the King was put in commission and it was arranged that the commissioners should be members of the legislative body to whom they are responsible'.[8]

The Cabinet depended upon a majority in Parliament and governed in the King's name and with his authority.

This solution was thought in the eighteenth century and much of the nineteenth to represent a division of powers. Not till Bagehot was it understood that in truth the Cabinet derived all its effective authority from Parliament.

From the eighteenth century the Cabinet was the seat of authority that could alone carry on the King's government—the sole place where legitimate political authority resided. In the Cabinet and in the Cabinet alone could decisions of government be made and registered that were accepted and executed by all the servants of the State.

A secret of the smooth adaptability of the British Constitution is that the Cabinet, which is central to the political life of the nation, is unknown to the law and thus extra-constitutional. Many constitutional changes and amendments that in other countries might have to be formally made are in Britain brought about by developments in the form and functions of the Cabinet. All that is necessary is that these developments should be accepted and carried on by successive Governments: often they may scarcely be noticed as constitutional innovations and may not be recognized and analysed until after they have passed into normal practice.

Because the Cabinet has continuously been the focus and fulcrum of politics, it has not been a passive subject of changes, simply adapting itself to the evolution of the political environment. The Cabinet of the 1950s and 1960s cannot be understood except in this light. Had the Cabinet been a different kind of organ with a different historical origin or continuity, the profound changes in the political environment in the last hundred years or so would have produced constitutional and political effects greatly dissimilar from those we know.

(2) Two-party System

The essential feature of the evolution of the political environment which reshaped the Cabinet and was refashioned by it was the emergence of a stable mass two-party system.

So much do we take for granted what is in fact a peculiar two-party system that we hardly feel the need to explain its emergence.

Myths are sometimes dressed up as explanations: such as the oblong shape of the chamber with a floor dividing it into two halves. The British Parliament has for many centuries had such a shape: but only for the past hundred years or so has there been a stable two-party system. As late as the days of Palmerston, Gladstone and Stanley 'crossing the floor' was comparatively easy.[9] The United States maintains two parties although both its chambers are semi-circular. Holland, alone of continental countries, has an oblong chamber but has never established a two-party system.

The method of election is more significant. Since the 1884–5 franchise reforms the pattern of a direct majority vote based on equal constituencies has favoured the two-party system by making it very hard for more than one of two parties to win a majority of the constituencies.

Such a system helps to maintain two parties, as was shown when Australia departed from it and introduced the preferential vote: the consequence was the rise of a third party, the Country Party.[10]

In Britain, as in other democratic countries, mass parties emerged in step with successive extensions of the franchise. In all these countries the outside parties were linked with parties in Parliament.

The normal continental pattern bore out Bagehot's forecast that a widened franchise would make the working of Parliament very difficult: for divergent interests produced a number of parties—a multi-party system.[11] But in regard to the country he was writing about, Bagehot was proved wrong.

Only in the United States and Britain, as full democracy was established, did a strong tendency towards a stable mass two-party system arise.

The essential feature that the two countries had in common was that the new mass parties fought for possession and control of already established sources of political authority—the Presidency and the Cabinet. Since each of these was the unique and sole seat of authority, no party could long survive that could not show itself capable of winning an outright majority. In terms of practical political logic only two parties could over a period of time be in such a position.

In America the fixed-term election of a President meant that the nation-wide parties were galvanized every four years into active existence. This in turn led to the characteristic and 'critical distinction between presidential party and congressional party'. American national parties are 'confederations of State and local party organizations (which) manage presidential nominations. All other public offices depend upon electorates confined within the States ... The President and Congressmen who bear one party label are divided by dependence upon different sets of voters.'[12]

In Britain the competition for control of the Cabinet, the unique source of authority, set up an equally strong tendency to produce two national parties. But the contest for the Cabinet was continuous and might be engaged at any time and not at set intervals. The resulting mass two-party system therefore became stable and continuous. Since the Cabinet was outstandingly the highest political prize in the country, rivalry between two parties involved the whole electorate in the main contention for political power. Both parties, whether in office or opposition, remained in permanent being.

The turning point for the emergence of mass parties in Britain was the 1867 Reform Act, which extended the franchise by eighty-eight per cent;[13] the Secret Ballot Act of 1872; the Corrupt Practices Act of 1883; and the Reform and Redistribution Acts of 1885. These together brought virtual manhood suffrage and constituencies of uniform size. The parties became increasingly dependent upon voluntary workers to canvass and get voters to the poll. The winning of a large number of constituencies became increasingly necessary. The number of contested seats rose abruptly—from 284 in 1859 to 442 by 1868; and then to 542 by 1880.[14] By the twentieth century virtually every seat was contested.

In 1867 Joseph Chamberlain founded the Liberal caucus in Birmingham, which had an accession of thirty thousand voters. Associations on the Birmingham model were set up in other large towns and in 1877 a Conference was called of ninety-three associations which launched the National Liberal Association.

Chamberlain claimed that the clean Liberal victory in the 1880 election was due to his new organization in the country. This assertion was of dubious validity.[15] But it was widely believed, especially by the defeated Conservatives. The readiness of each party to attribute an electoral reverse to inferior organization became one of the major factors impelling parties in a democratic system to imitate, outdo and again imitate each other. Party organization was thus driven to ever more complex and costly levels.

By the 1880s the Conservatives were tackling with their own weapons the Liberal Associations in Birmingham and other big cities. The Conservative National Union and the Liberal National Federation grew to resemble each other in essentials.

Simultaneously the parties in Parliament were transformed under the impact of two interacting factors.

The first was the now inescapable need to use the national parties to try and win a majority in Parliament. This made the party leaders — and thus the Prime Minister and the Cabinet — dependent on the electorate, rather than on Parliament.

The 1868 election was the significant turning point. After losing the election Disraeli resigned at once instead of waiting, as had been the previous practice, to meet Parliament. Gladstone behaved similarly on his defeat in 1874. Both assumed — as have all their successors — that it was now the electorate that made and broke Cabinets. The new practice became established only one year after the publication of Bagehot's book which took it for granted that Governments were normally fashioned and refashioned by Parliament.

The second factor was the competition between the parties for control of the Cabinet, now if possible *for the whole duration of a Parliament.*

This new phenomenon arose out of the need to put forward 'programmes' designed to stimulate the enthusiasm of party workers in the constituencies and to attract a majority of the voters. Such programmes required at least a whole Parliament in order to be carried into law.

To capture and hold the Cabinet called for a party with a clear and disciplined majority in the House. Normally only two parties could hope to be in this position. Thus the new contest for the Cabinet tended towards the emergence of two stable parties in Parliament and affected the organization and attitude of both of them.

Out of a Parliament with shifting and uncertain party loyalties, with many members whose prime concern was constituency matters or the pressure of vested interests—out of such a Parliament an institution had to be created that could enact a mass of new-type legislation to which the Government of the day and its party were committed.

By the mid-nineteenth century the concept and title of Leader of the House became first established. In 1869 the Government appointed the first regular parliamentary draftsmen.[16] Days were set aside for Government business.

The new concept of Parliament was voiced by Harcourt in a minute to the Cabinet in 1882: 'It is essential to secure to a majority the right to prevail which lies at the bottom of parliamentary institutions'[17]—historically a false view of Parliament, but in the new political environment a truism. The Cabinet pushed Harcourt's doctrine through the House and in 1882 the closure by simple majority was adopted.

The new powers of the Government in Parliament produced a new kind of Opposition. It became a party so organized that it could hope itself to become the majority with the rights ascribed to it by Harcourt. The party in opposition had to be as coherent and well-disciplined as the party in office. A Leader of the Opposition (first paid in 1937) faced the Leader of the House. The Cabinet was confronted by a Shadow Cabinet—a term that first came into use in the 1880s. In 1893 Long was charged by Balfour with looking after all questions in the House affecting his old department:[18] the first instance of a Shadow Minister. By the last quarter of the nineteenth century both parties had begun to put on the Whips for all important issues.[19]

The emergence of two organized parties facing one another across the floor of the House led to the need for a trusted and detached referee. Previously Speakers had been anything but impartial: they had, for instance, often spoken strongly and voted in Committee of the Whole House. The impartiality of the Chair began to be established under Speaker Shaw Lefevre who served from 1839–57.[20]

The duty of the Speaker came to be to see that neither party abused its position—that the Government with its majority got its way, but that the rights of the Opposition were not infringed. The Opposition became the residuary legatee of the time and the rights which had earlier been the prerogative of individual members, and which were increasingly transferred to the Opposition as a whole.[21] This process was taken to its logical conclusion in 1902 when Balfour carried new Standing Orders which appropriated for the Government the whole time of the House save for much curtailed opportunities for private members and twenty 'supply days' on which the Opposition could choose the subject of debate.[22]

Once two parties organized in this manner were in existence one Cabinet automatically and immediately replaced another. This came to be taken for granted as one of the advantages of the British Constitution.

Until a few decades before, delays had been frequent between one Government and another. When Whig Governments fell in 1851, 1852, 1855 and 1858, the Queen sent for Derby as leader of the largest group in Parliament. On each occasion he conducted negotiations with other leaders in a manner that remained characteristic of most continental democracies but was soon to disappear in Britain.[23] Bagehot spoke of 'the time now commonly occupied by a Ministerial crisis – ten days or a fortnight'.[24] The term 'Ministerial crisis' which came naturally to Bagehot's pen disappeared, in this sense, from the British political vocabulary.

The transformation of the Opposition was part and parcel of the transformation of the majority party – and just as significant: both were brought about by the contest for the Cabinet. The Opposition became the alternative Government because its leaders became an alternative Cabinet.

Two further steps were needed for the firm establishment of a stable mass two-party system in Britain.

The first was that the leader of each of the two parliamentary parties should become also the leader of his party in the country. Thereby these outside parties would be drawn into the two-party competition in Parliament for control of the Cabinet.

Gladstone was the first parliamentary leader to identify himself with his party in the country. In 1877 he went to Birmingham to give his blessing to the new National Liberal Federation. He was acclaimed as its leader and mouthpiece.

But Gladstone had still to reckon with Joseph Chamberlain who proclaimed at this same Conference his plan to form 'a truly Liberal Parliament outside the Imperial Legislature', which would formulate policy and control the actions of Liberal Members of Parliament.[25]

Joseph Chamberlain stormed his way into the Cabinet in 1880 after the great Liberal victory to which his new organization had contributed.

Chamberlain's resignation in 1886 over Home Rule led to a head-on battle between him and Gladstone for leadership of the National Liberal Federation. Chamberlain, its architect and previous hero, was defeated. Schnadhorst, the national agent and Chamberlain's close collaborator, together with the party machine, stood by Gladstone. Chamberlain formed the breakaway 'Radical Union', which won sixty-six seats in the 1886 election.[26] The strength of the tendency towards a two-party system drove Chamberlain and his Liberal Unionists into the Conservative Party within the decade.

Somewhat similar was the simultaneous revolt of Lord Randolph Churchill who tried to lead the Conservative National Union against the leaders in Parliament, claiming that it should take over 'the control of the party organization'. In 1882 Salisbury was sufficiently alarmed to speak of the danger that the House of Commons would become 'enslaved to the caucus'.[27] Randolph Churchill, like Chamberlain, stormed his way into the Cabinet. In 1886 he became the second man in it as Chancellor of the Exchequer and Leader of the House. He dropped his attempt to assert the claims of the National Union over the Parliamentary party, realizing that he was now a parliamentary leader himself. On his resignation from the Cabinet within a matter of months he had no outside support to challenge the leadership.

The national parties showed that they needed a leader round whom to rally and who could voice their aspirations: and that there was no other leader than the leader of their party in Parliament. The parties understood that they could hold their members together only if they got their programmes on to the statute book. This they could achieve only if 'their' party in Parliament got possession of the Cabinet. The linkage between party in Parliament and party outside Parliament involved the reproduction in the country of the two-party system that established itself in the House of Commons.

The new parties were necessarily broad groupings of people of differing views: otherwise each party could not have represented something like half the nation. The price paid for not having to form a coalition in a Ministerial crisis after an election was that the two parties, facing one another as Government and alternative Government, were themselves enduring coalitions, sometimes held together more perhaps by hatred of the other party than by love of all in one's own party: but held together also by broad policy, by loyalty, organization and leadership.

In these circumstances, tensions could arise within parties and between the party in the country and the party in Parliament. Occasionally a national conference could influence Government policy – as in 1926 when Baldwin's hand was forced on the Trade Disputes Act: though he had to contend also with strong views in his Cabinet in favour of such legislation. Government leaders, if united and assured of support in their party in Parliament, could ignore the views of a conference, as Baldwin did in 1933 when a resolution was carried against him on India.[28]

The second and decisive step needed for the firm formation of a stable two-party system was that the electorate itself should be drawn into the competition for the Cabinet and thereby into the acceptance and maintenance of a stable mass two-party system. If the people came to support as natural the rivalry between two leaders and two parties, then a third party would be likely to be eliminated: for there would be a very strong tendency for any political party to wither away or fail to establish itself in the first place that could not over a period demonstrate its capacity to form an alternative Government or a Government. This is the ultimate sanction, which only the electorate can impose, against more than two parties. The presence or absence of this sanction determines whether or not a country with universal franchise can have a stable and persistent two-party system and, if it is disturbed, restore it.

That the electorate had been drawn into the contest for the Cabinet was shown by the rise of the Labour Party. This was a new phenomenon in British politics—a party formed in the first place by forces outside Parliament. Since its purpose was to bring into being a party in Parliament, it would have been natural enough if the outside party had asserted its control over the party in Parliament.

This did happen in Australia with a very similar Labour Party in a very similar constitutional environment. In 1895 the party conference in New South Wales succeeded in subjecting the parliamentary party to its own caucus and compelling it to carry out policy laid down by the conference. On the formation of the Federal Labour Party in 1900 these compulsions were continued. In 1908 the Federal Executive resolved that all Ministers in any future Labour Cabinet should be elected by the vote of the parliamentary party. When the Fisher Labour Government was formed this procedure was followed and has been ever since.[29] A similar development occurred in the New Zealand Labour Party.

British Labour evolved on what had become normal British lines—though not without internal conflicts around this very issue.

Attempts were made from time to time to get resolutions through the Conference that would make the parliamentary party its creature—or, in the words of Mr Shinwell in 1920, its 'property'. In reply to Mr Shinwell, Clynes—chairman of the Parliamentary Labour Party—roundly declared: 'The Executive Committee has no authority over the Parliamentary Party.'[30] In 1928 Ramsay MacDonald told the Conference: 'As long as I hold any position in the Party they are not going to take their instructions from outside bodies unless they agree with them.'

Ramsay MacDonald was in 1922 elected the first leader of the Parliamentary Labour Party: till then the title had been chairman. He and his successors were accepted, as in the other two parties, as leaders of the whole party, inside and outside Parliament—with the right, should the party win enough seats, to become Prime Minister: as MacDonald did in 1924.

The rise of the Labour Party for a time disrupted the established two-party system. So shrewd an observer as Asquith wrote in 1926: 'In my judgment, the Third-Party system has come to stay.'[31]

In other European countries this was the pattern that established itself after the rise of socialist parties – an extra party was permanently added to the political constellation.

But, deep in the British political environment, so strong were the forces making for a stable mass two-party system that within two decades Labour displaced the Liberal Party. Once the Liberals lost the ability to form even an alternative Government they rapidly withered away. A new two-party system established itself.

In 1960 the Labour Party faced the same conflict for ultimate authority between the party in Parliament and the party in the country that the Liberals and Conservatives had solved in the 1880s.

The 1960 Conference carried a resolution against the parliamentary leaders on the major issue of unilateral nuclear disarmament. Hugh Gaitskell, the leader of the party, defied the Conference and the Parliamentary Labour Party stood by him. In the following year Conference reversed its decision. In October 1968 Mr Harold Wilson as Prime Minister ignored a five to one defeat of the Government's prices and incomes policy – although he accepted the reverse as a 'warning' to the Government.

The evolution of a stable mass two-party system was a British solution to the challenge of universal suffrage which might well have Americanized or continentalized the party system: and thus Cabinet and Parliament.

The decisive factor in this evolution was that the Cabinet remained throughout the sole source of political authority.

As the central prize of the political battle the Cabinet was the major force making for a unique mass two-party system which proved more stable than during most of the nineteenth century when the franchise was more restricted. The Cabinet itself grew stronger as the result of the changes that it helped to bring about.

The secret of the political and constitutional evolution of Britain in the century down to the 1950s and 1960s was not the passing but the survival of the Cabinet.

PART TWO

Evolution of the Cabinet

FOREWORD

During the last century or so the Cabinet underwent, in response to changes in the political environment, an evolution in regard to its conduct, its structure, its composition, its status and its mode of operation.

This evolution was an adaptation to, and itself a factor in, the democratization of political society: and may be called the democratization of the Cabinet.

I consider this process in the following four chapters—nos 2 to 5.

In all but two of the matters I deal with, a clear pattern of evolution can be detected. But in regard to the counting of heads in the Cabinet and the co-ordination of departments, it is not yet possible to say whether this is equally true. There are indications of an increasing tendency for heads to be counted and for Cabinets to be dominated by departmental interests: but it may be that we are here dealing not with long-term or trend changes, but with variable practices that go to and fro from time to time.

The trend or enduring changes in the Cabinet—a body of which the law is ignorant—effected considerable alterations in constitutional practice: some of them gradually, some quickly.

CHAPTER 2

CONDUCT OF THE CABINET

(1) Voting in Cabinet

Whether or not heads are counted in Cabinet seems to depend to a considerable degree upon the Prime Minister and the measure of unity of the Administration. Prime Ministers and other Ministers may feel in different degree a need to shelter behind Cabinet decisions that involve and commit all the members.

Melbourne, in 1841, counted heads on whether to dissolve Parliament. Gladstone – particularly in his disparate and divided administration of 1880–85 – counted heads as a fairly regular practice: in 1881 the decision to arrest Dillon was taken by the Prime Minister's casting vote. Lord Granville rebuked Gladstone in 1886: 'You too often counted noses in your last Cabinet.'[1]

In 1902, Salisbury counted heads on three or four occasions. In the same year under his successor, Balfour, there were many votes on the Education Bill: the decision to limit it to secondary education was taken by ten votes to eight.[2]

Asquith says, 'It was not in any of the Cabinets in which I have sat, the custom (unless in exceptional cases not always of the first importance) to take a division.'[3] Asquith himself was perhaps the clearest example of the opposite of a head-counter. He saved Lloyd George's Budget of 1909 when a vote would have defeated it overwhelmingly. Of another instance Lloyd George said, 'They were all against it and they all said so; and then Asquith rubbed his chin and said: "I think the balance of argument is in favour" and put it through. He did that lots of times.'[4] On two occasions Lloyd George took a vote: once, apparently, to forestall an intervention by Churchill on a matter concerning pictures.[5] (See Chapter 6, p. 100.)

27

Amery, who served in Cabinets under Bonar Law and Baldwin, said that the Prime Minister might occasionally take a vote but 'this is the exception, at any rate on issues of major importance'.[6]

In my recollection Attlee, whilst he did not draw the Asquithian distinction between 'balance of argument' and 'balance of opinion', hardly ever counted heads.

I can recall only two occasions when noses were counted in Attlee's Cabinet — once on a relatively trivial matter in order to save time: as it happened, the vote was a tie and Attlee, amidst general laughter, gave his casting vote. The second occasion was the great crisis of the Cabinet in April 1951 over charges on the Health Service (of which I give an account in Chapter 9). In fact Morrison was in the chair as Attlee was absent ill. Perhaps Attlee would have avoided a vote; but he would not have found it easy.

Neither Eden nor Macmillan[7] ever counted heads. Occasionally they would go round the table and ask each Minister individually for his views. If opinion seemed evenly divided the matter would be postponed for further consideration. If only one or two were against a proposition, they would be asked to accept the majority view. If a major Minister — such as the Chancellor — dissented, he would be asked to think over his position.

Mr Harold Wilson fairly frequently went round the table. On a number of occasions he openly kept his own tally of the votes pro and con; and sometimes announced the result.

On one occasion an important issue of domestic policy was reached by a majority of one or two votes.

(2) Co-ordination of Departments

A Cabinet consists primarily of heads of departments. Gladstone was to this extent stating a truism when he said, 'The Government must in this country be a Government of Departments.'[8]

'Co-ordination' can take various forms. It can simply mean that the Cabinet acts as a kind of court of appeal between Ministers, each of whom primarily looks after the interests of his own department and regards it as his main role in the Cabinet to ensure that these are not damaged by the interests of other departments. Or it can mean that departmental views and concerns are woven into a unified and dominant Government policy and that Ministers consider their major duty to be to partake in the formulation of this policy.

In practice all Cabinets exhibit departmental co-ordination of both kinds: but there is sometimes a clear leaning one way or the other.

Under North fragmentation of policy went very far. He inherited a system under which, after Chatham's death, the Cabinet was reduced to a collection of independent departments without a head. North said, 'I found it so and had not the vigour and resolution to put an end to it.' During its twelve years' course his Government was, in his own words, 'a government by departments, the whole was done by the Ministers, except in a few instances'.[9] Pitt and Peel were strong Prime Ministers who themselves dominated the departments.

Of Gladstone's later and less united Cabinets, Harcourt complained that the Prime Minister 'regarded Heads of Departments as autonomous'.[10] Salisbury deplored that under Disraeli 'the chiefs of departments got their way too much. The Cabinet as a whole got it too little.'[11] Haldane, who confessed that he 'ought to have taken a more active part in the general business of the Cabinet', said that 'the Cabinet of 1906 in its later years was like a meeting of delegates'.[12]

In my own experience Mr Harold Wilson's Cabinets were perhaps more ones of departments than Attlee's; though at most the difference was one of degree only. The prolonged discussions on the Common Market in Mr Wilson's Cabinet were a very striking example of the putting of general policy above departmental interests.

My own attitude as a Minister always leaned to the view that the loyalty and interest of each member of a Cabinet is to its policy as a whole. I can recall how surprised and even angry Dalton was on one occasion in 1951 when, as Commonwealth Secretary, I argued in favour of ending our subsidy to the sea passage of British emigrants to Australia—the last remaining example of such a practice. To Dalton it seemed that I was failing in my duty as a kind of representative of each Commonwealth country in the Cabinet. To myself it seemed that I should decide my advice to my colleagues in part in accord with what

I regarded as this country's long-term interest, in part in the light of the Chancellor's pressure for economies in Government expenditure and only in part in terms of Australia's views.

Mr George Isaacs, Minister of Labour, who had no close departmental interest, argued strongly on the other side. In the end a compromise was reached by which the subsidy was reduced, though not abolished.

A conflict of departmental interests of a sharp kind arose in the long Cabinet discussions early in 1968 on large savings on proposed Government spending. As Secretary of State for Education I did not conceive it as my sole or prime duty to fight all out and at all costs in defence of my departmental Estimates as they stood. Each department in my view had to try and forward the Government's collective policy by agreeing to accept economies as great as were compatible with the maintenance and, in due course, the renewed advance of the social service concerned. Having secured a considerable scaling down in the original proposals for a four-year postponement of the raising of the school-leaving age and for cuts in capital investment in the universities, I agreed to lesser reductions in both these expenditures as being on a par with those made in defence and the other social services and necessary, with these other savings, to reach the desired target of economies. This attempt to take a governmental and not merely a departmental line was not popular amongst all departmental Ministers and was attacked by some of them. About half the Ministers in charge of spending departments took a line similar to mine. The proportion, I understand, was about the same in post-war Conservative Cabinets, when similar issues arose.

(3) Collective Responsibility

The doctrine of collective responsibility—that every member must accept and if necessary defend Cabinet decisions even if he opposed and still dislikes them—this doctrine was not in the beginning part of the Cabinet system. In George III's time Ministers sometimes spoke and even voted against policies determined by the Cabinet.[13]

As the two-party system began to arise so the feeling grew that such behaviour was improper. With the full establishment of the mass two-party system the doctrine of collective responsibility passed into the unwritten conventions of the Constitution – something that every-one took for granted. The doctrine was indeed necessary to the Cabinet from the mid-nineteenth century onwards. Cabinet Ministers were party leaders: both their leadership and the party itself would be weak-ened if the leaders openly attacked one another or publicly attributed views to one another.

The high-water mark of the concealment of difference was in 1859 when the Derby Cabinet was sharply divided over a proposed Reform Bill. Two members resigned in late January: but, in order to preserve appearances, continued to attend Cabinet meetings and delayed their open resignation and their explanations to Parliament till March 1st.[14]

An inevitable concomitant of collective responsibility was the disclosure of internal Cabinet affairs. Often this was authorized: as when a Minister gave guidance about a White Paper or some policy in an off-record press conference. This was regularly done by the Leader of the House to the Lobby conference after his announcement in the House of business for the following week.

Some disclosures were unauthorized. These are often described as unattributable leaks.

The unattributable leak must be distinguished from the disclosure of true state secrets – such as the details of a budget, a decision to devalue, military or security matters. These have been scrupulously observed: apart from Dalton's inadvertent disclosure, the only example of a breach of security was the betrayal by J. H. Thomas of budget secrets in 1936.

The unattributable leak involves the disclosure of other matters that are secret only because of the doctrine of collective responsibility – such as the subject of Cabinet discussion, Cabinet decisions, views assigned to different Ministers and the like. The leak gives information known only to members of the Cabinet; being unattributable, it does not breach the doctrine that Ministers do not attack one another in public.

An element of concealment was inherent in the very concept of collective responsibility. The doctrine that the Cabinet must appear to be united presupposed Cabinet divisions that had not been reconciled. Ministers must in the nature of things have differences but they must

31

outwardly appear to have none. Collective responsibility must therefore to some extent be a mask work by the Cabinet.

The self-same conditions of mass democracy that gave rise to
collective responsibility produced the unattributable leak. The maintenance of secrecy imposed by the doctrine became intolerable. This
for two main reasons.

First, Ministers were political creatures living in a political world.
As party leaders they accepted the need for the doctrine of collective
responsibility: but as political creatures they felt it sometimes necessary
to let their political views be unofficially known.

Secondly, the press began to try and tear away the mask from the
face of the Cabinet: their readers became increasingly interested in
being informed about 'secrets' that were felt to be of a political and not
a security nature. Already by the mid-nineteenth century one newspaper kept a man stationed in Downing Street to report the length
of Cabinet meetings and any persistent absentees.[15] By the present
century a corps of Lobby correspondents was maintained to report on
political events, which included the unattributable leak.

The beginning of the unattributable leak can, perhaps, be dated back
to 1880. In that year Lord Salisbury in a letter to Balfour described
collective responsibility as a 'constitutional fiction'.[16]

It became generally known that in the Liberal Administration of
1880–85 various Ministers maintained special relations with particular
newspapers and fed them information in order to prepare the ground
for an argument in Cabinet.[17]

From then on the unattributable leak became a feature of the
Cabinet system. One of the most extraordinary examples was in 1923
when Bonar Law did not conceal from the American Ambassador his
anger at the settlement of Britain's debt to the U.S.A. just concluded by
Baldwin, his Chancellor of the Exchequer: and then published in *The
Times* an anonymous attack on the policy decided upon by the
Cabinet.[18] *At least the Editor of *The Times* must have known his
identity.

Ministers often did not give unattributable information direct to a

* See Chapter 5, p. 92.

newspaper, but talked fairly freely to M.P.s in the smoking-room or tea-room of the House of Commons: such information often made its way to the press. This happened in both Labour and Conservative Cabinets from the end of the second world war onwards. The main motives for leaks by Ministers were: the hope of gaining support from a particular newspaper or correspondent; the desire to inform – or perhaps mislead – their supporters in the Parliamentary party or the country about the stand they had taken in the Cabinet on a particular issue; the attempt to mobilize party or public opinion behind a view that was being argued in Cabinet. On occasion a newspaper might invent a leak in whole or in part.

After the second world war the appointment of a Press Secretary attached to the Prime Minister made the leak in a sense normal and almost official: for one of the Press Officer's duties was to brief political correspondents about Cabinet meetings. At first such briefing was limited to information about which members were present; which Ministers had been invited to attend; and, perhaps, a hint of the subjects discussed.

As time went on, there was a tendency to give a special emphasis or angle to these briefings or to omit some aspect of the meeting.

Some official light was for the first time thrown on these briefings in April 1969 – ironically enough in connection with an alleged assertion by the Prime Minister in strong terms of the necessity for collective responsibility.

In the whole national press on April 5th, 1969 appeared closely similar accounts of remarks said to have been made to the Cabinet by Mr Harold Wilson following a vote by Mr Callaghan, the Home Secretary, on the National Executive Committee of the Labour Party against a Government White Paper which had been approved by the Cabinet.

When questioned in Parliament, the Prime Minister stated that he had authorized this disclosure to the press with the consent of the Cabinet: 'where the Cabinet agrees to information being made available, then from that moment it is no longer regarded as an official secret.' (House of Commons, vol. 782, cols. 1156–7.)

All the newspaper reports contained verbally similar remarks regarding the 'skilful, resourceful and tough' approach by the Prime Minister: that, said Mr Harold Wilson, was 'a matter of press construction' (ibid.).

This was only one of a number of disclosures (before as well as during Mr Harold Wilson's time) that must necessarily have emanated directly or indirectly from the Prime Minister—many of them certainly without Cabinet consent. Other Ministers were stimulated thereby to give the press their version of what had happened.

In post-war Conservative Cabinets when a leak seemed to involve disclosure of the contents of an official paper or Minute, the Cabinet Secretary would be asked to check on how many officials had had access to the document. Ministers were not questioned.

Similar checks were sometimes made in Mr Harold Wilson's Cabinets. On a number of occasions the question of particular leaks was somewhat angrily discussed after being brought up either by the Prime Minister himself or by another Minister. Sometimes the Prime Minister charged the Lord Chancellor to inquire into the source of a leak. The Lord Chancellor would find out how many people in various departments had handled a document and would send for and question Ministers. Nothing ever came of these investigations. Many Ministers —including myself—resented being questioned by a colleague and made their feelings clear. During 1968 these inquiries became less frequent and finally ceased.

Thus the doctrine of collective responsibility and the unattributable leak grew up side by side as an inevitable feature of the Cabinet in a mass two-party system. In every Cabinet the leak will be deplored and condemned; but it is paradoxically necessary to the preservation of the doctrine of collective responsibility. It is the mechanism by which the doctrine of collective responsibility is reconciled with political reality. The unattributable leak is itself a recognition and acceptance of the doctrine that members of a Cabinet do not disagree in public.

Salisbury was right to describe collective responsibility as a *constitutional* fiction. Its maintenance is constitutionally essential. If members of a Cabinet publicly attacked one another, a Cabinet based on a system of two disciplined parties could not be sustained. The leak is the price paid for the maintenance of a constitutionally necessary doctrine.

That is why the 'agreement to differ' over a major issue of policy in January 1932 was an aberration or blind alley in Cabinet evolution. Snowden, Samuel, Sinclair and Maclean—in order to avoid their resignation over the introduction of tariffs—were allowed to vote and speak against particular proposals of a Government of which they remained members. Had it become established that Cabinet 'unity' could no longer be preserved by the timely leak, but only by public and open disagreement on a number of matters, then the whole Cabinet system would have been undermined.

(4) Size, Composition and Frequency

Down to the first world war the Cabinet grew steadily in size as fresh departments were created or older departments grew in importance. In the last quarter of the nineteenth century, a new post of Secretary for Scotland (later Secretary of State) was created and a Board of Agriculture set up: the Board of Education, the Local Government Board and the Post Office acquired increased importance.[19] Ministers in charge of lesser departments were sometimes omitted from the Cabinet: but the principle was accepted that the heads of all significant departments should be in the Cabinet in order that departmental interests could be represented and co-ordinated.

Thus, as the number of departments grew, so correspondingly grew the Cabinet. The eighteenth-century Cabinet had from five to nine members; during the greater part of the nineteenth century there were from twelve to fifteen members; the five Cabinets before the first war averaged nineteen members, rising to twenty-three under Asquith.[20]

The two world wars apparently interrupted this process. Very small Cabinets, it was thought, would enable urgent day-to-day decisions to be speedily taken. Lloyd George's War Cabinet consisted of from five to six members. In fact large numbers of people were invited to attend, not all of them Ministers. The average attendance of non-members was half a dozen, rising, when a highly controversial issue was at stake, to an extra twenty. Sometimes there were as many as thirty-five present. In 1917, 248 different people attended the War Cabinet meetings and in 1918, 278. The War Cabinet could, however, and on occasions did, meet as a small body—in effect a high-powered committee of the normally larger Cabinet, capable of taking decisions.[21]

Lloyd George's post-war Cabinet had twenty members. The heads of six major departments, created during the war, were excluded: but all these Ministries were abolished in the next few years.[22]

Further offices were created and by 1939 Neville Chamberlain's Cabinet was back to twenty-three.

Winston Churchill's War Cabinet had seven to eight members: but a number of 'constant attenders' in practice swelled the size of the Cabinet.

The critical and definitive changes came in 1945. Although some departments were abolished, such as the India Office and the Burma Office, many new Ministries were now in existence—Labour, Health, Transport, Defence, Power, Pensions, Welsh Affairs. In addition some non-departmental Ministers were needed to chair Cabinet Committees and co-ordinate various fields of activity. For the first time in conditions of peace, a Prime Minister found himself with more Ministers than could fit into a Cabinet. This problem was made the more acute because Attlee managed to keep his Cabinet relatively small. He was therefore the first Prime Minister to leave a large number of Ministers out of his Cabinet—no less than twelve.[23]

At the same time the process of reducing the number of peers in the Cabinet was carried further. This development reflected the shifting balance of power between the two Houses and made more room for leading Ministers in the Commons.

In the 1850s and 1860s the pattern had been one of equality between peers and commoners. Gladstone used Whig peers to balance radical House of Commons Ministers. In 1885 Hartington remarked that 'there is one thing in which I agree with Harcourt, which is that the Peers ... cannot expect half the places in another Liberal Cabinet.' In the three Liberal Cabinets after 1892 the proportion of peers was under a third. Salisbury and Balfour had nine or ten peers in their Cabinets. After 1906 the proportion of peers fell away.[24]

Attlee's Cabinet of 1945 had only four peers out of twenty members. Churchill in 1951 made a brief return to the older Conservative practice with six peers out of sixteen members. Macmillan's Cabinet of 1962 contained three peers.

There is no statutory provision as to the number of peers to be included in the Cabinet. The House of Commons Disqualification Act, 1957 (as amended to February 15th, 1968), provides that not more than ninety-one Ministers can sit in the House of Commons. 'Ministers' for this purpose include Under Secretaries of State and Parliamentary Secretaries.

Thus it would legally be possible for a Prime Minister to have as few peers in his Cabinet as he wished by putting the necessary number of non-Cabinet and junior Ministers in the Lords.

There was a steady increase in the total number of Ministers. In 1939 the figure was fifty-nine. Attlee in 1945 raised the number to sixty-six and it remained slightly above this level under Churchill and Mr Macmillan. In 1964 Mr Harold Wilson sharply raised the number to ninety-eight.

Mr Wilson was therefore under a statutory obligation to have seven Ministers in the Lords. In fact in 1964 he had only two peers in his Cabinet. This was the lowest number until then — and the lowest possible number as long as it is assumed that the Lord Chancellor must be a member; since the Leader of the Lords must clearly be in the Cabinet.

The net effect of these changes was to prevent a continual rise in the size of the Cabinet. However, a factor on the other side came increasingly into play — namely the tendency towards 'representative' Ministers — that is Ministers who were held to speak for and represent important outside interests. When the Minister of Education was left out of Churchill's 1951 Cabinet there was an outcry amongst educationists. Mr Harold Wilson, speaking in the House of Commons on November 21st, 1968, declared that a Prime Minister could not leave out of account the representative aspect of certain Ministers: 'It is inconceivable that the important sectors of our national life, and particularly those employed in and concerned with those particular sectors, should have only a secondary level Minister not in the Cabinet.'

Prime Ministers tend to favour a large Cabinet for another reason. 'A large Cabinet helps a Prime Minister to control his senior colleagues' by enabling him to appeal against them to minor members of the Cabinet. Austen Chamberlain complained of this practice by Lloyd George.[25]

Thus, after an initial drop in size, Cabinets began to grow larger again. Attlee kept his Cabinets down to seventeen or eighteen. Churchill's Cabinet of 1951 started with sixteen members but rose to nineteen by December 1955. Mr Macmillan started with eighteen in 1957 but had twenty-one Cabinet Ministers by 1962. Mr Harold Wilson's Cabinets averaged twenty-three members—the size of Neville Chamberlain's Cabinet of 1939 and Sir Alec Douglas-Home's in 1964.

Meanwhile a series of amalgamations reduced the number of departments. The Ministry of War Pensions was absorbed into the Ministry of Pensions: later Pensions was merged with the National Assistance Board to make a Ministry of Social Security. The Admiralty, War Office and Air Ministry were absorbed into the Ministry of Defence. The Commonwealth and Colonial Offices were merged. In 1968 the Commonwealth and Foreign Offices were amalgamated, as were the Ministries of Health and Social Security.

In consequence by 1968 there were only two departments outside the Cabinet—Overseas Development and the Ministry of Public Buildings and Works: apart from the Post Office, which was soon to become a public board.

The press of business led to a steady increase in the frequency of meetings. Before 1914 the Cabinet met about forty times a year: between the wars about sixty times: since 1964 about ninety times a year.[26] As we shall see, there was at the same time a great increase in the number of meetings of Cabinet Committees.

CHAPTER 3

ORGANIZATION OF THE CABINET

(1) Inner Cabinets

The term 'inner Cabinet' is a misnomer. It is in no sense a Cabinet and must be distinguished from a Cabinet Committee. An inner Cabinet has no organic or set place in the Cabinet structure: it is no more than an informal, small group of friends or confidants of the Prime Minister drawn from members of his Cabinet. It is not formally set up; it has no papers or records; it is not served by the Cabinet Secretariat. An inner Cabinet as such has no power, no place in the hierarchy of political authority. It may, amongst other things, discuss questions coming before the Cabinet; but only to concert the advice the members of the inner Cabinet will tender to their colleagues. An inner Cabinet does not and cannot predigest the business of the Cabinet; nor set it aside or duplicate its work.

In regard to such a loose and informal thing as an inner Cabinet, the practice of Prime Ministers varies according to their predilections and perhaps the balance of opinion in the Cabinet. Some Prime Ministers have not felt the need for an inner Cabinet.

In his post-war Cabinet Lloyd George first had an inner Cabinet of Horne, Geddes and Greenwood. In 1921 these had been displaced by Churchill and Birkenhead. In 1938 Neville Chamberlain had an inner Cabinet of Simon, Halifax and Hoare—which was well enough known to be dubbed the 'Big Four'.[1]

Equally MacDonald's inner Cabinet in 1923-4 was known as the 'Six'—Henderson, Clynes, Snowden, Thomas and Sidney Webb. In 1930 the 'Big Five'—the above less Webb—met regularly in the Prime Minister's room. These were minority Governments and the purpose of MacDonald's inner Cabinets was general discussion about the parliamentary situation, the state of the Labour Party and the tactics to be pursued in the House.[2]

Attlee in his first Administration made use of an informal inner Cabinet that consisted of Bevin and Cripps and, sometimes, Morrison. After the deaths of Cripps and Bevin, Attlee did not find close confidants among his Cabinet colleagues and became rather aloof.

Eden and Macmillan had no inner Cabinet. Each talked often to one or two individual Ministers about matters that concerned them and which might come to Cabinet.

Mr Harold Wilson in his early days as Prime Minister had an informal inner Cabinet – made up of Mr George Brown, Mr Callaghan and myself. We met on a number of occasions at Chequers: when we came together at No. 10, other Ministers were sometimes present.

We discussed such matters as whether to devalue, whether to raise Bank Rate, whether to impose an import surcharge.

In the interval between my leaving the Cabinet in January 1965 and rejoining it in 1967 Mr Harold Wilson had abandoned consultation with an inner group of Ministers.

(2) Cabinet Committees

As distinct from informal inner Cabinets, Cabinet Committees were very early set up to discharge a function on behalf of the Cabinet: they have therefore partaken of the authority of the Cabinet. One of the ways in which the Cabinet adjusted itself to the pressures of the mass two-party system was by an ever-increasing formality and precision of Cabinet Committees.

The first step was the setting up of ad hoc committees of Cabinet Ministers for the expedition of business. One of the earliest examples was the 'War Committee' set up in 1855. It consisted of the Prime Minister, the Secretary for War, the First Lord and the Home Secretary and considered various matters concerned with the Crimean War. All decisions had to be endorsed by the full Cabinet. Other examples were the committee of five Ministers set up in 1870 on the use of the Suez Canal in wartime and the committee on the defence of Constantinople in 1878.[3]

As the pressure for legislation grew in the second half of the nineteenth century, committees were set up, usually under the responsible Minister, to draft Bills. After 1892 this procedure was made more systematic. The autumn Cabinets decided on the Bills for the coming session and the more important of these were handed over to drafting committees. Officials and draftsmen, though technically not members, worked closely with Ministers on these committees.[4]

In 1903 Balfour created the first standing committee – the committee of Imperial Defence. It was not strictly confined to Ministers: Balfour, for instance, served as a member from 1906–15 whilst in Opposition. But the essential business was done by four or five Ministers. The Committee of Imperial Defence was the first Cabinet body to have a secretariat. Asquith appointed committees to consider Edward VII's Civil List and Lords Reform.

During the first war very many committees were set up in a haphazard way. Whilst Asquith was Prime Minister some of these were established by the Cabinet and some by Ministers on their own authority without consulting the Cabinet. Asquith asked Lord Hankey to co-ordinate their functions. He found that as early as August 20th, 1914 there were twenty committees: by December 1916 the number had risen to 102. In two years Lloyd George set up sixty-three committees: by then the total was 165. Amongst these committees were: Trading with the Enemy; Restriction of Enemy Supplies; Diversion of Shipping; Trade and Supplies.[5]

All committees disappeared on the return of peace save for the Committee of Imperial Defence and the Home Affairs Committee which was primarily concerned with drafting Bills, not with their merits. In 1920 a standing Finance Committee was set up.[6]

Between the wars a good many ad hoc Cabinet Committees were appointed; in an average year some twenty were in existence: amongst these were the Irish Situation Committee and the Economy Committee; and committees on House of Lords Reform, the Publication of Secret Documents, Agricultural Policy and on Iron and Steel.[7] Of this period it has been said: 'There existed many committees, but hardly a committee system.'[8]

The committee on unemployment under J. H. Thomas created by the Labour Cabinet in 1930 was significant because of a new departure in connection with it—namely, the establishment of a committee of officials to service it. This system was greatly developed in the 1930s and became a permanent method for speeding up the transaction of business under Ministerial control.[9]

In the second world war, as in the first, a full-fledged committee system was developed, but a more coherent one. This system became the basis for peacetime Cabinets from the end of the war onwards.

On June 4th, 1940 Attlee gave the House of Commons a detailed account of the structure of Cabinet Committees. (House of Commons, vol. 361, cols. 769–70.)

He described the composition of the Defence Committee under the chairmanship of the Prime Minister and went on to list the five committees dealing with economic and home affairs. These were:

(i) The Production Council (Chairman, Minister without Portfolio).

(ii) The Economic Policy Committee (Chairman, Minister without Portfolio).

(iii) The Food Policy Committee (Chairman, Lord President of the Council).

(iv) The Home Policy Committee (Chairman, Lord President of the Council).

(v) The Civil Defence Committee (Chairman, Home Secretary).

Supervising these five committees was a steering or planning committee under the chairmanship of the Lord President of the Council.

Churchill on January 22nd, 1941 gave the House further information. (House of Commons, vol. 368, cols. 261–4.) The full membership of the Steering Committee was disclosed: as well as of two further committees called the Import Executive and the Production Executive.

The most important of these wartime committees was the Home Affairs Committee (which went under different names at different times). It became responsible for a major part of domestic policy. The 1944 Education Bill, the Government's most important piece of legislation, was settled in this committee and, as all the members and therefore the relevant departments were agreed, it did not go before the Cabinet.[10]

Here was a striking example of a new principle in the Cabinet system: namely that a Cabinet Committee was parallel to and equal with the Cabinet. Within its jurisdiction and subject to possible reference to the Cabinet, a committee's conclusions had the same force and authority as those of the Cabinet itself.

In 1945—in contrast to 1918—the wartime system of committees was continued. Attlee was thus the first Prime Minister to have in peacetime a permanent structure of Cabinet Committees. He re-organized and simplified the committee system that he had inherited. In one category came the committees chaired by the Prime Minister himself. Attlee presided over the Defence Committee (which had during the second world war displaced the Committee of Imperial Defence), the Economic Policy Committee and the Nuclear Defence Committee.

In another category came committees presided over by other Ministers—sometimes the Minister principally concerned; sometimes co-ordinating Ministers without a department, like Morrison, Green-wood and Addison. The basic structure was as follows:

The Legislation Committee was responsible for allowing and supervising the drafting of Bills and determining the order of their introduction into the House: the Future Legislation Committee planned ahead for several sessions. An Economic Planning Committee was created with the task of overseeing planning, manpower and allied matters. A Production Committee looked after more short-term problems. An Agricultural Policy Committee was responsible for working out the annual Farm Price Review.

This set free the Home Affairs Committee to consider the merits of all proposed Bills and other matters which did not fall to another committee or were not important enough to be taken direct to the Cabinet. In addition Bills due to go to the Cabinet in any case often came first before this committee.

By these means the merits of Bills and policies were considered

43

before they came to Cabinet: some were settled in committees; committees were also responsible for the first draft of Bills, White Papers and the like.

Attlee introduced committees of junior Ministers presided over by a junior Minister to consider matters not of primary political importance. I chaired one such committee to keep Russian communist propaganda in various parts of the world under review, and to take or recommend counter measures.

The pattern established by Attlee was continued by subsequent Conservative Prime Ministers and became the standard structure of the Cabinet system of the 1950s and 1960s. Under the Conservatives the Prime Minister presided over the Defence Committee: the Chancellor of the Exchequer over the Economic Policy Committee; the Home Secretary over the Home Affairs Committee; and the Leader of the House over the Legislation Committee.

Mr Macmillan put the Agricultural Policy Committee under a non-departmental Minister instead of the Chancellor of the Exchequer so that there could be an arbiter between the Treasury and the Agricultural Departments over the Farm Price Review.[11] When I was Minister without Portfolio I chaired this committee.

Mr Harold Wilson himself presided over the Overseas Policy and Defence Committee and the Steering Committee on Economic Policy (set up in July 1966).

Other committees established by Mr Wilson were the Prices and Incomes Committee and the Social Services Committee (which further reduced the burden on the Home Affairs Committee).

The original type of ad hoc committee continued to be used alongside the organized structure of standing committees.

In 1951 during the Abadan crisis the Cabinet, which was meeting very frequently, delegated full powers between its meetings to the Prime Minister, the Foreign Secretary and the Chancellor of the Exchequer. They were authorized in emergency to take decisions in the name of the Cabinet. A Malaya Committee was set up to watch over day to day developments of the communist insurrection in that country. Mr Harold Wilson similarly appointed a Rhodesia Committee.

Something of a return was made to the principle of the drafting committees of the later nineteenth century which were attended by officials. A sub-committee of the Social Services Committee was set up in 1966 under Mr Crossman's chairmanship to work out a new wage-linked Superannuation Bill; and the following year a Committee on Lords Reform: on both these committees officials served with Ministers. The Committee on Lords Reform, after a number of meetings in which divergences of view had appeared, decided to have a day-long session at Chequers and came to unanimous conclusions to recommend to the Cabinet.

The Prime Minister sets up and disbands committees, appoints the chairmen and members and sets the terms of reference. Normally, besides the Ministers departmentally concerned, some other Ministers are put on committees to ensure that policies are broadly considered. Ministers can be represented by their junior Ministers. Often a non-departmental Minister is in the chair: indeed a Cabinet today needs some such Ministers for this purpose—probably about four.

Considerable arguments and even dispute can arise over these matters. A Minister may consider that his prestige or his departmental interests are involved: where various departments have overlapping interests there may be competition for the chairmanship of a key committee.

A major innovation made by Mr Harold Wilson was to raise the authority of Cabinet Committees.

Under Attlee and his Conservative successors many matters that were considered in a committee went afterwards to the Cabinet and were discussed over again. Any Cabinet Minister who did not get his way on a committee could, and often did, ask to have the matter referred to the Cabinet.

In 1947 the Cabinet rejected all the main proposals of the Economic Planning Committee.[12]

In Mr Harold Wilson's first Cabinet the right of appeal from committee to Cabinet still prevailed. In 1964 I and one other Cabinet

Minister insisted on taking a question from the Overseas and Defence Policy Committee to the full Cabinet.

In 1967 Mr Harold Wilson informed the Cabinet of his view that a matter could be taken to the Cabinet from a committee only with the agreement of the chairman. In exercising his discretion the chairman would consider the degree of disagreement in the Committee or the intrinsic importance of the issue or its political overtones. In cases of dispute the question could be brought to the Prime Minister himself. Although this did not take away the constitutional right of a Cabinet Minister to bring any matter to the Cabinet including a question settled in a committee, in practice this right was greatly attenuated. This considerably reduced the pressure of business in the Cabinet.

The value and appropriateness of the committee system from Attlee's time was demonstrated by the fate of the attempt made by Churchill, when he succeeded Attlee in 1951, to introduce Overlords charged with the duty of co-ordinating a number of related departments.

The Opposition at once pointed out that responsibility of Ministers to Parliament was blurred. Who was to answer for policy, the departmental Minister or the co-ordinating Overlord? In April 1952 Lord Woolton said that the Overlords were responsible to the Cabinet and not to Parliament. By August 1953 Sir Winston Churchill abandoned the idea. 'Now that we are in smoother waters', he announced, 'we can rely on the normal methods of Cabinet procedure to secure co-ordination between the departments ...'[13]

By 'normal methods' Churchill meant the committee system dating from 1945. It had by now become the natural and accepted way of running Cabinet government. As with many constitutional innovations, including originally the Cabinet itself, an attempt was made to cast a veil of secrecy over Cabinet Committees. They came, however, to form so essential and structural a part in the working of the Cabinet that secrecy gradually broke down. It became widely felt that the public had a right to know at least the organization of the Cabinet system, which was the seat and centre of political authority in the country.

The 'Parliamentary Committee' set up by Mr Harold Wilson in 1968 is hard to classify. It possessed some of the characteristics of a Cabinet Committee. It consisted of about ten Cabinet Ministers presided over by the Prime Minister: other Ministers were called in when matters concerning their departments were under discussion: it was serviced by the Cabinet Secretariat with the usual agenda and conclusions. But it had no clear scope or terms of reference of the kind given to a normal Cabinet Committee. Its declared purpose was to enable a smaller part of the Cabinet to consider general political and parliamentary problems: it thus carried out some of the functions of an 'inner Cabinet' but was far too formal for such a group. In some respects it resembled a 'partial Cabinet'. (See Chapter 5, p. 88.) In so far as this smaller group had effective power, it meant that for some purposes the Cabinet was smaller: this, as we have seen, involved a diminution in the Prime Minister's actual authority. (See Chapter 2, p. 38.) No essential change was made when, on April 29th, 1969, Mr Harold Wilson announced that the membership of this 'committee' would be reduced from about ten to about seven.

One judgment passed on the Parliamentary Committee is that it 'was evidently more of an expedient to help the Prime Minister than an administrative innovation'.[14]

It seems extremely improbable that successor Cabinets will continue this experiment. Neither the Parliamentary Committee nor its successor is, therefore, likely to enter into the regular structure of the Cabinet system.

Mr Crossman regards the evolution of Cabinet Committees as one of the factors in the 'passing of Cabinet government'. 'The point of decision ... was now permanently transferred either downwards to these powerful Cabinet Committees or upwards to the Prime Minister himself.'[15] Much the same point was made in another work in 1957 — about the effect of the careful preparation of papers by Cabinet Committees: 'Much Cabinet business is now almost formal.'[16]

In fact the committee structure enabled a great deal more work to be transacted by Ministers: it permitted these to concentrate more than before on the co-ordination of policy between their own and other departments. The Cabinet was left freer for the more important decisions: much of the work that came before it was now better prepared. Sometimes, as for instance in the consideration of a White Paper that had come up from a committee, the Cabinet's work might be formal: but there was always some formal business before every Cabinet. Far the greater part of the Cabinet's work was anything but formal. Concentrated as it now was on the more significant issues, there could be prolonged argument before decisions were come to. Any matter of great importance that had been considered by a committee was brought before the Cabinet and on occasion a different decision made.

The preparatory papers and Minutes of every committee (except some that are considering secret matters) are circulated to Ministers who can if they wish raise points about them: though it must be added that the flow of paper is so great that a Minister often does not read these papers. However, his department will draw a Minister's attention to any matter that concerns it: and the Prime Minister, aided by the Cabinet Secretary, keeps an eye on the papers.

The committee system puts a great strain upon Cabinet Ministers who spend much of their working day at committees. But it greatly relieves the burden on the Cabinet. Present-day business could not be transacted by the Cabinet, were not much of the work delegated to committees.

The committee system not only enables Ministers not in the Cabinet to join in the settlement of policies on issues that relate to their departments: it also allows junior Ministers, in a way that was not possible before, to learn something about the working of the Cabinet system.

Above all, the use of committees has increased the efficiency of the Cabinet, without reducing its oversight and control over policy decisions.

(3) Cabinet Secretariat

The origins of the Cabinet Secretariat can be traced back to 1903 when, under Balfour, a Foreign Office clerk was assigned to keep the Minutes of the Committee of Imperial Defence. Campbell-Bannerman set up a system of sub-committees which became in time very elaborate: and the size and importance of the Secretariat grew. It prepared agendas, kept Minutes and provided a link between the departments concerned.[17]

At the opening of the first war the Secretariat began to establish a closer connection with the Cabinet. It served as the secretariat to the War Council set up by Asquith in November 1914 consisting of leading Ministers: for secrecy's sake the Minutes were kept in manuscript. Asquith, however, refused to have a Secretary at the actual Cabinet. He held this to be in conflict with 'established constitutional doctrine and practice'.[18]

In 1916 Lloyd George broke down this last scrupulous barrier and created the Cabinet Secretariat. Ten Assistant Secretaries were added to the Secretariat; and it served both the Cabinet and all Cabinet Committees.[19]

On the restoration of peace the Cabinet Secretariat came under sharp criticism. In a House of Commons debate in June 1922 speakers denounced it as unconstitutional and in the General Election of that year Bonar Law, though somewhat equivocally, promised to abolish it. As Prime Minister he found the Secretariat too useful to get rid of. But its size was drastically cut from 144 to 28 – partly because of the abolition of almost all wartime Cabinet Committees: and partly because of the transfer of some of its functions to other departments.[20]

The method and activity of the Cabinet Secretariat in the 1950s and 1960s was established under Attlee.

The Secretary, in consultation with the Prime Minister, prepares the agenda for the Cabinet. In Attlee's day this could be a very important matter. The agenda tended to be overloaded and items low on it were often not reached perhaps for a week or two. Ministers with matters on which they wanted an urgent decision might ask the Secretary or the Prime Minister to put an item higher on the agenda. Other Ministers might have contrary views. The Prime Minister, if necessary, decided such disputes.

These things could still happen under Mr Harold Wilson, but his delegation of enhanced authority to chairmen of Cabinet Committees considerably lightened the Cabinet agenda.

The agenda together with papers relating to the items on it are sent by the Cabinet Secretariat to the Private Offices of Cabinet Ministers with references to past relevant papers, which are kept in conditions of special secrecy in the Private Office. It is the duty of the Private Secretary to get together all the papers needed by his Minister for a Cabinet meeting.

In the Cabinet the Secretary and his two assistants keep longhand notes to aid them in the preparation of the Conclusions (as the Minutes are called).

It seems that in George III's time the Cabinet recorded a formal Minute of its proceedings to be sent to the King. Between 1779–82 the Minutes became so standardized that they may have been drawn up by a clerk. The last such Minute was sent in 1839. Already in 1837 the Prime Minister had already begun to send a personal letter to the King about discussions in the Cabinet. This remained the practice for seventy years. Ministers did not see the Prime Minister's letters to the King and had to rely on their memory about Cabinet decisions: on several occasions recollections differed.[21]

In 1916 the Cabinet Secretariat began to keep Minutes of Cabinet meetings and of less formal meetings of Ministers. The Secretary and Assistant Secretary took notes of discussions. At first the Minutes fully set forth the course of the discussion, mentioning Ministers by name. In 1921 the record became briefer: Ministers were named only at their express wish. At the same time, in the interests of greater secrecy, the Minutes ceased to be printed. In theory distribution of the full version was restricted to the King and the Prime Minister, other Ministers receiving letters of reminder on items that particularly concerned them: but (as Thomas Jones explains) in practice the Cabinet Secretary used his discretion and some Ministers always got all the Minutes. By 1924 it had become the practice to circulate the Minutes to all members of the Cabinet.[22]

Thereafter little change occurred. In their present form the Conclusions are designed not so much as a record of proceedings but rather as instructions for action to departments. Ministers are referred to by the title of their office and the only ones so mentioned are those who have submitted papers to the Cabinet and, occasionally, a Minister who is closely concerned in the item of business. When the Prime Minister sums up, he too is mentioned by title. The conclusions are always in *oratio obliqua*. Where there is argument, the points made are briefly set out without any reference to actual speakers. The purpose is to give enough of the argument to elucidate the conclusions reached. Where the conclusions involve action by a Minister he is not instructed but 'invited' to take the necessary measures.

In order to give an idea of the form of the Minutes I append the conclusions of an imaginary Cabinet meeting:

(iii) Driving on the right of the road.

The *Minister of Transport* said that the overwhelming argument for changing the rule of the road was that this must be done sooner or later and the longer it was put off the more expensive the change would be. When the Channel Tunnel was built the change would be inescapable. The cost would be very considerable and the Home Affairs Committee had examined various possible ways of raising the money—such as a special lottery or a temporary surcharge on the cost of motor car licences. Even if the Cabinet agreed to make the change the delay would still be considerable, since many new road signs would have to be manufactured and some major alterations made in junctions and roundabouts. This was a reason for speedy decision. He recommended the Cabinet:

(1) to take the decision in principle to change the rule of the road. Such a decision would help to accustom the public to the change.

(2) to agree to carry out this change at the earliest possible moment.

(3) to set up a committee to work out how soon the change could be made.

[NOTE. *This part of the Minute may be based more on the paper put in by the Minister than the, possibly brief, remarks he made in introducing it.*]

The *Chancellor of the Exchequer* said that, while he agreed with the idea in general, this was certainly not the moment to make the change. The cost would, at a time when the Cabinet wanted to keep down public expenditure, be unacceptably high. In any case much closer estimates of the cost were needed. He did not agree that postponement would increase the real cost: it might do so in money terms; but the cost to the nation was in terms of manpower and materials.

Proposals for raising the necessary money called for most careful consideration in the light of the economic situation. He recommended the Cabinet to postpone indefinitely consideration of the matter.

[NOTE. *This might be either a summary of the Chancellor's remarks or of a paper if he had put one in.*]

In the course of discussion it was argued that it was politically important for Britain to adapt itself as quickly as possible to continental standards and practice: there was considerable pressure in Europe for us to make the change. It would help our motor car exports if we could produce left-hand drive cars both for the home and the European market. It would reduce ultimate costs to make the change before embarking on the new programme for extending the motorways.

On the other hand it was said that, whereas many other changes, such as decimalization, were desirable and practical, this change was so colossal an undertaking as to be of quite a different order. Different rules of the road, as a divisive factor in Europe, mattered less in the case of an island than between continental neighbours. The Channel Tunnel still seemed as far off as ever.

[NOTE. *This is the normal way of recording the middle and main part of the debate. The Minutes give no indication of the order in which the points were made: they are always marshalled pro and con. There is no way of telling who spoke or even how many Ministers spoke. Not all the points made in argument are recorded. No indication is given of the tone or temper of the debate.*

The *Prime Minister,* in summing up the discussion, said that there were still considerable differences of view on this very important question. He thought there was a broad measure of agreement in favour of taking a decision in principle to make the change. A clear majority of the Cabinet envisaged that the change would have to be made sooner or later. He himself thought that the balance of argument was in favour of announcing such a decision in principle. There was no agreement about making the change as soon as possible. He proposed that the Minister of Transport's suggestion of a committee to examine the best timing for the change should be accepted. The committee should also look more closely into the costs.

The *Cabinet decided:*
in principle to change over to driving on the right-hand side of the road.

The *Cabinet invited* the Minister of Transport:

(a) to arrange to inform Parliament of the decision;

(b) to arrange for a committee of officials to examine the timing and cost of the change-over.

The *Cabinet invited* the Minister without Portfolio to arrange, after the committee had reported, for the matter to be considered again in the Home Affairs Committee.

Since the Conclusions are the official embodiment of Cabinet decisions, Ministers may sometimes have a word with the Secretary to try and ensure that the conclusions of a perhaps not wholly clear discussion contain the points they wish. Very occasionally the Conclusions are challenged in the subsequent Cabinet meeting. Disagreements are determined by the Prime Minister.

One or twice in Attlee's Cabinet Mr Bevan requested that his dissent from some decision should be recorded in the Minutes. The same thing occasionally occurred in subsequent Conservative Cabinets. It would in fact be impossible to record a Minister's dissent from a Cabinet decision: for this would amount to a disagreement with his colleagues of such a nature that he would have to resign.

The Conclusions are sent as soon as possible to departments.

In cases where urgent action is needed, such as the despatch of a telegram to an ambassador or the movement of troops, the Secretariat may ring up a department on a specific Conclusion.

On one occasion, in 1923, Baldwin asked the Cabinet Secretary to withdraw during a sharp dispute amongst Ministers on protection.[23] Once or twice Attlee asked the Cabinet Secretary and his colleagues to withdraw whilst party political matters were discussed. I cannot recall Mr Harold Wilson doing this: indeed so complete had become the confidence in the discretion of the Cabinet Secretariat that sometimes party political matters were frankly and even sharply argued in the presence of the Cabinet Secretary. I understand that this is what happened in Conservative Cabinets. Such discussions are never referred to in the Minutes.

The Cabinet Secretary keeps a full index of Conclusions with a network of cross references.[24]

Some Conclusions of great secrecy are kept by the Secretary in a special annexe to the Minutes. This is recorded in the Minutes and Cabinet Ministers may consult the annexe if they wish.

The Cabinet Secretariat serves all Cabinet Committees in exactly the same way as the Cabinet itself: agendas are drawn up; papers circulated; and Conclusions recorded and distributed to departments.

Whereas the Prime Minister fixes the time for meetings of the Cabinet and the committees over which he himself presides, the times and places of other Cabinet Committees are fixed by the Secretariat without consulting the chairman of the committee. This is because the fitting in of times and meeting places, so that they do not overlap one another or involve a Minister being in two places at once, is a complex jig-saw puzzle.

Apart from the Cabinet Secretary himself, the Secretariat is recruited by secondment from departments. There is rivalry amongst these to send their ablest people. In 1969 the total staff amounted to 108: but this included miscellaneous officers whose duties had little or nothing to do with the working of the Cabinet. The number directly servicing the Cabinet and its committees was about forty-five. These included the Secretary, a Deputy Secretary, three Under Secretaries, five Assistant Secretaries and ten Principals.

Conclusions of both Cabinet and committee meetings are sometimes clearer and fuller than the discussions they record.

On one occasion when I was chairman of a Cabinet Committee I thought that the last item on the agenda was one on which all the members, having read the papers, would be in agreement. Without calling on the Minister to present his paper I asked whether any member had any comment to make. As there was silence, I declared the item to be agreed. When the Conclusions were circulated, the Minister's paper was set out at length together with his recommendations and it was recorded that these had been agreed to. This was necessary so that a proper record could be made and to enable appropriate action to be taken by the departments concerned. Occasionally I have known the same thing to happen in Cabinet.

One of the most important developments of the Secretariat is that the Cabinet Secretary has become something like a Permanent Secretary to the Prime Minister. The Prime Minister has no department: but the Cabinet Secretary helps him in much the same way as the Permanent Head of a department would help his Minister. When Lloyd George was absent for many months in Paris in 1919, the office of the War Cabinet (as it was still called) had its headquarters in Paris too.[25] As Mr Harold Wilson put it in a television programme in 1964 before he became Prime Minister – 'The Cabinet Secretariat would provide advice for the Prime Minister on what might be going wrong and on policy.'[26] He briefs the Prime Minister on items on the Cabinet agenda, including papers put in by Ministers. He may suggest lines of argument that the Prime Minister may wish to pursue. He draws his attention to important points in the agenda or Conclusions of Cabinet

Committees. He generally advises the Prime Minister on matters of policy, on disputes between departments and the like.

The Secretary makes recommendations for changes in the committee structure—such as the setting up of new committees or bringing existing ones to an end, or the rearrangement of terms of reference to avoid overlap between committees.

It is very easy for committees to proliferate and, if this is not carefully watched, time may be wasted instead of saved.

In 1950 during a period of active rearmament and economic stress a great many committees were set up. An inquiry that year revealed the existence of over a hundred Cabinet Committees, many of them with overlapping functions. A special co-ordinating section was set up in the Cabinet Secretariat with the remit to 'follow the work of the many committees dealing with defence and economic questions and to ensure that there is no duplication; in cases of doubt to suggest which particular committee should consider a particular question; and generally to see that the new problems emerging are dealt with smoothly and efficiently'.[27]

Today the Cabinet Secretariat attempts to deal with this kind of problem currently in the advice that the Secretary gives to the Prime Minister.

A senior member of the Secretariat similarly helps the chairmen of committees. Written (and sometimes oral) briefs are given to them on each item of the agenda, together with suggested lines that they might consider taking.

The Cabinet Secretariat in the 1950s and 1960s underpinned the whole structure of the Cabinet system. It kept the Cabinet and the committees in mesh. It provided the cog wheel between decisions taken in Cabinet or committee and the departments of State: between the decision and the execution of policy. The Cabinet Secretariat enabled speed and clarity of execution to be achieved in an enormous press of business.

CHAPTER 4

CONSTITUTIONAL STATUS OF THE CABINET

The evolution of the Cabinet in line with the changing political environment brought about a significant shift in the interrelationship between the Cabinet and the other major factors in the Constitution – Crown, Parliament and Civil Service.

(1) Cabinet and Parliament

The *Cabinet in Parliament* is the central feature of the British Constitution.

The Cabinet is not – as Bagehot thought – a committee of Parliament. Rather it is 'the activating and leading part of Parliament'.[1] It is the collective leadership of the majority party in the House of Commons. Through, and to the extent of, its control of this party the Cabinet exercises control over Parliament.

Its power to do so was enhanced by the changes in the structure and machinery of the Cabinet system,[2] which we considered in the previous two chapters.

The Legislation Committee (which decides which Government Bills, and in what order, should be introduced during the Session) together with Government disposition of the time of the House gives the Cabinet mastery over legislation in Parliament.

This extends to private as well as public Bills. The Legislation Committee considers all business brought forward by private members, both Bills and motions. The committee determines whether to oppose them, to let them run on or to block them. The question of giving Government time for a controversial private member's Bill is discussed by the Cabinet itself. It does not take a decision upon the merits of the Bill; division of opinion on a controversial Bill would show itself also in the Cabinet and if the Cabinet took a stand one way or the other, some Ministers might find it necessary, on a point of conscience, to resign.

The whole question is whether time should be given. However, time is not provided unless there is a marked desire for the passage of the Bill in Parliament, in the party and in the Cabinet. If time is given, the vote is a free one and Ministers can vote as they wish.

The detailed management of Parliament from day to day is secured by the weekly discussion in the Cabinet of the business for the following week, including debates initiated by the Opposition. It is the formal prerogative of the Chief Whip to decide whether to put on the whips and, if so, whether to back them with the authority of a three-line whip. But he acts as one of a number of colleagues bound by collective responsibility. He will be influenced by the views expressed in Cabinet: on occasion the Cabinet will itself take a decision about whipping. In practice the Cabinet and the Whips operate as a single whole.

On a number of occasions a Cabinet has insisted on reversing a defeat in the House of Commons: Balfour announced such a decision in 1905; Asquith, in 1912; and Churchill, in March 1944.

Through the establishment of a stable two-party system the Cabinet in Parliament evolved to the point, by the 1950s and 1960s, at which it exercised, on behalf of Parliament, some of the latter's previous functions.

As early as 1867 Bagehot observed that Cabinet and not Parliament controlled public expenditure. He pointed out that 'the House of Commons ... has long ceased to be the checking, sparing, economical body it once was. It is now more apt to spend money than the Minister of the day ... In truth a Cabinet ... must have the sole financial charge.'[3]

Public expenditure continued to grow rapidly. In Bagehot's day supply expenditure amounted to four per cent of the gross national product: by 1962 it had risen to twenty-five per cent.[4] This increase was largely due to the extension of the social role of the State which went with the widening of the franchise. Ministers responsible for 'spending' departments acquired something of the propensity to spend that Bagehot had discerned in the House of Commons.

Gradually the Cabinet evolved within itself conventions that enabled it to control public expenditure.

In 1869 formal Treasury supervision of the Estimates was established: a circular was sent from the Cabinet to all departments directing them to communicate with the Treasury before announcing any policies that would involve a charge upon the Exchequer.[5] In 1872 accounting officers were appointed by the Treasury to check detailed expenditure and estimates in each department.

Owing to the conflict between the Treasury and the spending departments, Chancellors found themselves on a number of occasions in difficulties with the Cabinet over their attempts to check expenditure. In 1886 Randolph Churchill resigned after his defeat on the Estimates. On the same issue Gladstone as Prime Minister resigned in 1894. In January 1958 Mr Thorneycroft with all his Treasury Ministers resigned when the Cabinet rejected some of his proposals to prune the Estimates.

In January 1968 the firmness of the Prime Minister and the Chancellor of the Exchequer was a vital factor in carrying through the Cabinet the considerable programme of savings in public expenditure.

By degrees, though not without difficulty, the authority of the Chancellor in these matters began to grow within the Cabinet. His chief means of control was through the budget.

The budget in its modern legislative form dates from 1859. Before that year, taxes had been introduced in separate Bills and dealt with by the Cabinet as they came up. Often full discussions took place on specific tax proposals. In 1859 – in order to frustrate the Lords who had rejected a Bill on the paper duties – all taxes were consolidated into a single Finance Bill. The Chancellor's complete proposals came before the Cabinet in one statement.

Cabinet Ministers did not easily forgo their previous right to discuss tax changes. Gladstone had to fight hard for his budgets of 1860 and 1861. In 1885 the Cabinet asked Childers to postpone his statement to the House so that it could alter some of his proposed duties. In 1886 Randolph Churchill had to discuss in Cabinet for months in advance a budget that he never introduced owing to his resignation on the Estimates. In 1894 Harcourt had a row with Rosebery, the Prime Minister, over death duties. He circulated to some of his Cabinet colleagues the memoranda that had passed between himself and

Rosebery.[6] In 1900 one of Hicks-Beach's proposals was rejected and in 1902 he offered the Cabinet a choice of three different ways of raising the extra revenue he needed.[7] Lloyd George's budget of 1909 was considered in fourteen Cabinet meetings from mid-March to April 19th, budget day.[8]

Between the wars a new practice gradually evolved in the Cabinet which resulted in the tacit delegation of its authority over the budget to what can be described as an informal committee of the Prime Minister and the Chancellor.

The practice became established in Cabinets of all parties that the Chancellor should, in consultation with the Prime Minister, work out his budget on his own and submit it to the Cabinet a day or two before opening his budget in Parliament The only Ministers to have prior knowledge are those with whom the Chancellor will discuss the parts of his proposals that directly affect their departments.

This development was primarily due to a change in attitude in the Cabinet rather than to pressure by Chancellors of the Exchequer. Members did not wish to be burdened for too long by heavy and dangerous secrets: a view that was strengthened by J. H. Thomas's betrayal of budget secrets in 1936. Another reason was the realization that Government economy and control of expenditure would be better secured than if the Chancellor's proposals were subject to detailed scrutiny by a Cabinet in which spending departments were well represented. The Cabinet remains collectively responsible for the budget and could, if its members wished, revert to the previous practice of long discussion of tax changes.

I cannot recall any serious attempt by Attlee's Cabinet to do this. Hugh Dalton in 1945, following a discussion in the Cabinet after he had outlined his budget, increased personal income tax allowances by more than he had originally intended. This necessitated a rush job to reprint all the tables.[9] Once or twice in post-war Conservative Cabinets the form and presentation, though not the substance, of the Chancellor's budget statement might be altered after his disclosure of its details to the Cabinet. The discussions in 1951 concerned only a small part of Mr Gaitskell's budget and arose out of a deep division in the Cabinet.

The shortness of the notice given by the Chancellor was questioned by one or two Ministers in Mr Harold Wilson's Cabinets—more particularly by Mr Crossman. The Chancellor was strongly backed by the Prime Minister and most of the Cabinet.

An analogous practice developed in relation to changes in Bank Rate. The tradition that such changes should not be discussed in the Cabinet arose in the nineteenth century because the Bank was an independent institution. The Bank of England Act 1946 brought Bank Rate under the control of the Government. The rule against Cabinet discussion was maintained: no longer to protect the independence of the Bank, but to give the Chancellor rights similar to those he had acquired in relation to the budget.

In September 1957 Mr Thorneycroft's proposal to raise Bank Rate to seven per cent was disclosed beforehand to the Cabinet since it formed part of a parcel of connected measures. The Cabinet, however, decided to leave the decision in regard to the Bank Rate, in the usual way, to the Prime Minister and the Chancellor. [10]

The Cabinet nearly always meets on a Thursday, which is the day when, traditionally, alterations in Bank Rate are announced. The Chancellor tells the Cabinet of any change that he has decided upon at twelve noon precisely, the hour when the City and the world is informed. Should the Cabinet not be meeting on the relevant Thursday there is no way of informing the Ministers and they—like everyone else—discover the news from press or radio.

Thus by the 1950s and 1960s the Cabinet, in order to control finance on behalf of Parliament, had voluntarily forgone its rights in regard to changes in Bank Rate and in taxation.

The Cabinet took Parliament's place as the object to which interested groups and associations directed their main attention.

Whilst M.P.s were still relatively independent of the control of the Cabinet and the Whips, vested interests worked directly upon them. The wealthier and better organized pressure groups maintained regular support for themselves in the House.

Bagehot spoke of the 'jobbing propensities' of Parliament and wrote that 'there are said to be 200 "members for the railways" in the present Parliament' (that of 1866–8).[11]

In 1860 Gladstone feared that so many members were connected with the paper industry that he might lose his proposal to alter the paper duties. In fact the Government majority fell from fifty-nine to only five. Disraeli used to refer to the West Indian interest in the House as the 'sugar members'.[12]

The identification of the Cabinet with Parliament and the organization of party discipline through the Whips had the effect that vested interests concentrated their efforts upon the Government and the departments. This was to the benefit of both parties: the interests were concerned to bring influence to bear where decisions were made; the Government, as policy became more complex, found consultation necessary.

By 1885 Gladstone was ready to enter into direct negotiations with pressure groups—particularly the brewers. By the 1930s the Government began to help associations to form. The first chairman of the Iron and Steel Federation, which was set up in 1934, was appointed by the Government. Similarly the Government helped to establish the Woodland Owners' Association in 1956. Once an association had established a continuing relationship with the Administration, the Government would often help it to resist any attempt to organize breakaway groups: as, for instance, in the case of the British Legion in 1943.[13]

Consultation with interest groups became a structural part of the technique of government. 'The Ministry of Food ... always dealt with the trade associations in formulating the basis of policy' (1949): 'Statutory instruments are almost always framed after consultation with the parties concerned' (1953).[14]

In some cases a statutory duty was laid upon a department to consult the relevant interests. For example the Agricultural Act of 1947 imposed an obligation on the Minister to consult 'with such bodies of persons as appear to him to represent the interests of the producers in the agricultural industry'. A similar provision was laid down in the Industrial Organization and Development Act of 1947.[15]

Individual M.P.s, as they became more susceptible to the control of Whips, won a relative immunity from pressure groups. It was said in 1961 that when a conflict arose between loyalty to the Whips and the interests of a group with which a member was closely associated — M.P.s usually gave 'their voices to the groups and their votes to the parties'.[16]

After the second world war attempts to influence M.P.s began to be made by public relations agencies paid by overseas Governments. Sometimes special visits and trips, often on a lavish scale, were arranged. The number of members involved in such activities was very small: the number who were influenced, smaller still. The House, however, became uneasy and in 1969 demands were made that agencies acting for overseas Governments should be required to register and that the register should be public.

Although interests still found it or thought it worth their while to keep contact with particular M.P.s, the House had become a very different place from that described a century before by Bagehot.

The exercise by the Cabinet of some of the functions of Parliament is an aspect and consequence of the Cabinet's control over, and therefore identification with, Parliament.

But this does not imply an arbitrary rule. The 'Cabinet in Parliament' means that the Cabinet is in a very real sense a part of Parliament. All Ministers emerge from the back benches: all may and some do return to them.

The Cabinet in its discussions continually takes into account the probable reactions in Parliament. Major concern is with opinions inside the Government party in the House — naturally enough, since the Cabinet must be alert to maintain its majority. The broad divisions in the party are reflected in the Cabinet itself because a Prime Minister in forming his Administration must take into account the balance of views within the party. The argument that 'our fellows won't stand it' can be as persuasive in Cabinet today as it was when Morley in the 1890s used it to Lord Rendel.[17]

In various Governments the Cabinet's hand has occasionally been forced by a concealed mobilization by the Prime Minister or other Ministers of the opinion of a section of the Party: such mobilization can be competitive, as on one occasion in Mr Harold Wilson's Cabinet.

Attendance by the Prime Minister and other Ministers at meetings of the parliamentary party 'upstairs' – that is in a committee room on the first floor of the Palace of Westminster – is a major feature of the management of the party by the Cabinet. Cabinets sometimes test out party feeling before finally coming to a decision: but both parties, when in government, are careful not to disclose to a party meeting Bills and other matters that should first be told to Parliament. The Leader of the Opposition and the Shadow Cabinet similarly attend and manage party meetings upstairs.

Sometimes pressure on the Government by the parliamentary party may be enough to influence it. In 1957 a committee of the Conservative 1922 Committee pressed for an amendment of the Rent Act, which was in fact introduced the following year.[18]

More often the pressure exerted on the Government is a mixture of opinion expressed in the party meeting upstairs and of speeches, abstentions or hostile votes in the House. In 1947 Attlee told the party meeting that an eighteen-month period of conscription was necessary: the proposal was carried, but against a substantial opposition. Soon after, seventy-two Labour M.P.s voted against the Bill embodying this proposal and many abstained. The Cabinet then told a party meeting that it had decided to reduce conscription to twelve months.[19]

The Opposition and Parliament as a whole can influence the Cabinet, which is very conscious when the Opposition is doing well, winning by-elections, advancing a policy that appears to be moving public opinion. 'In practice the deliberation of a Government is profoundly influenced by the anticipated reactions of Parliament and the public.'[20]

In 1951 the Labour Cabinet agreed to the appointment of an American admiral to command the NATO fleet in the Atlantic, including a number of British ships. It was shaken by the intensity with which public opinion seemed to be supporting the protests of the Opposition. At this point Australia informed us that it wanted with the

United States and New Zealand to form the ANZUS, from which Britain was excluded, and that it would like our consent to this procedure. As Commonwealth Secretary I pointed out that this was an act of Australian sovereignty and that any delay on our part would be against the spirit of the new Commonwealth. However, the Cabinet was scared of another 'American admiral' case and there was a very considerable delay, during which Australia made some heated protests, before I was authorized to say that we had no objections.

Cabinets often, indeed nearly always, decide to go ahead despite opposition in their own party. The Conservative Cabinet in 1954 withstood a lot of pressure in the 1922 Committee against the decision to leave the Suez base. Churchill addressed the Committee and carried its reluctant acquiescence.

Sometimes it can be a close run thing to get a policy through the House. Mr Heath in March 1964 defeated an important amendment to his Resale Price Maintenance Bill by only one vote. The Labour Government in 1968 had greatly reduced majorities in securing the passage of its Prices and Incomes measure.

In the 1950s and 1960s abstentions and hostile votes by sections of the Government party became a fairly constant feature of Parliament. On some occasions the Cabinet gave way, as in April 1969, when the Bill to reform the House of Lords was withdrawn. But in general the authority of the Cabinet remained, because the objectors did not want, in their own and the party's interest, to defeat the Government or to damage it too much in public esteem.

The Cabinet gets its way: but not simply by an order of the Whips.

The Cabinet in Parliament is a reality. The Cabinet dominates Parliament: but it is always conscious of it and wary of it.

(2) Cabinet and Civil Service

The simple dichotomy between Legislature and Executive does not apply to Cabinet government.

If these two organs are to check and balance one another, there must be a division of powers between them: they must be separate and distinct. The Cabinet is in Parliament and of it. Therefore both

E   65

Cabinet and Parliament are very different from the 'executive' and the 'legislature' in the American sense of these terms.

Parliament cannot function as a legislature without the Cabinet which prepares and drafts Bills and uses its majority to get them through: and (as we have seen) also controls the fate of private members' Bills.

Equally Parliament cannot alone bring the decision-making process under political control. To ensure that responsible politicians and not civil servants have the final say, Parliament needs the supplementary aid of the Cabinet acting on its behalf.

The decision-making process has become extremely complex. In response to the demand for social and welfare legislation the Civil Service has grown steadily in size. In 1914 the administrative class (that is to say, civil servants who share in policy making) had 500 members. By 1955 the number had risen to 3,500.[21] The non-industrial Civil Service – which makes decisions in regard to innumerable rights and duties of citizens – grew between 1964–8 from 413,000 to 474,000.

Numerically, the vast majority of administrative decisions affecting individual people have to be made by a large number of civil servants without the knowledge of a Minister. For example, in the National Insurance system in 1957, thirty thousand officials dealt in a year with ten and a half million claims for unemployment, sickness and maternity benefit and paid out four and a half million retirement pensions.[22] The considerable increase made by Mr Harold Wilson in the number of Ministers of State and junior Ministers subjected a wider field of decision-making to Ministerial control. But the problem remained that detailed administration had become so vast and multifarious that it could not be brought under close Ministerial supervision. The only method of control was to lay down as carefully as possible the broad lines of policy within which the administrators worked: but this, except in regard to major policies, had necessarily to be done by higher civil servants.

Ministerial control is made easier by the attitude of civil servants, whose whole instinct is to obey and carry out their Minister's policy and, if necessary, to try and elicit one from him. On entering office on a number of occasions I always found that senior civil servants, whilst preserving silence about the methods and confidences of my predecessor, were eager to discover and execute my policy. They regarded it as their duty to keep the whole department in line—and those in lower posts looked for a lead from above.

Ministers themselves are responsible for many decisions that are not subject to further control. Within departments, especially those with a large number of junior Ministers, the Minister in charge has to lay down the division of responsibility. Having done so, he often has no further control over what is decided: though, if he is wise, he will have frequent meetings with his junior Ministers.

The supreme control of decision-making is in the Cabinet and its committees. Although they are backed by no legal sanction, Conclusions of the Cabinet or, within its jurisdiction, of a Cabinet Committee take precedence over other decisions in any part of the executive and are carried out as a matter of course by Ministers and civil servants.

In practice there has been a certain growing together of Cabinet and Civil Service. The tendency, as old as the Cabinet itself, for a Minister to identify himself with the continuing policy of his department became stronger. Departmental Ministers often appeared in the Cabinet as champions and spokesmen of their offices. A neat and striking example was in Asquith's Cabinet: in 1910, Winston Churchill, as Home Secretary, led the attack upon the demand of McKenna, First Lord, for more ships; by 1913 they had exchanged offices and each, with equal conviction, maintained the opposite view.[23]

Close co-operation between a Minister and his Private Secretary is essential to proper control of a department: it is mainly through the Private Office that a Minister makes his views known through the department. Out of this co-operation a 'Private Secretaries' network' arose, including the Private Office at No. 10. This facilitated and short-circuited the dispatch of business. It provided a useful means of communication at a discreet level between Ministers. If one Minister wished to convey an attitude or concern to another without directly approaching him, he could get his Private Secretary to ring up his colleague's Private Secretary to indicate his own observation about his Minister's views.

A more recent and more important reason for the growing together of Cabinet and Civil Service was an extension of the system that grew up in the 1930s of servicing Cabinet Committees by corresponding official committees. The Cabinet itself began to be serviced, for certain purposes, by official committees, often at the level of Permanent Secretaries of departments.

The relations between Ministers and officials were affected by the evolution from a departmentalized to a unified civil service. Until 1919 civil servants tended to remain all their working life in one department: in that year a single service was created within which officials could be transferred between departments. Promotions were controlled by the Treasury and Permanent Heads of departments and their deputies could be appointed or removed only with the consent of the Prime Minister. This was at most a minor factor in raising the status of the Prime Minister; but it had an effect upon the Civil Service which will be reinforced by the changes made in 1968. Control was then removed from the Treasury to a new Civil Service Department under a Minister working under the Prime Minister.

The consequence of these developments has been the gradual rise of a collective view in the Civil Service, particularly among leading officials. One example of this is the practice of Permanent Heads of departments to hold regular meetings together. Senior civil servants tend to form collective views about the merits of Ministers; this can affect their prospects, especially in the case of junior Ministers. Equally Ministers tend to form collective views about leading civil servants.

On the whole Ministers, the Cabinet and Cabinet Committees manage to exercise political control over a very wide field of decision-making, including all important decisions. But, in doing so, they are themselves operating as part of the decision-making process outside Parliament.

Therefore the second role of the Cabinet is vital to the political control of decision-making—namely that of being answerable to Parliament as the apex of the executive. The discharge by Cabinet and

Parliament of this role depends upon the maintenance of the doctrine that Ministers are responsible for policy and civil servants for executing it. Even though this distinction is not as clear-cut as once it was, its consequence—namely that only Ministers and not civil servants can be called to account—is essential to Parliament's contribution to the political control of the executive: for on this doctrine rests the right of Parliament to question a Minister on any facet of his responsibilities. This power often helps a Minister to exercise more effective control over the mass of detailed decisions for which he is responsible, though unaware of them. Aggrieved citizens turn more naturally to M.P.s than to the department and more profitably. A letter from an M.P. goes directly to the Minister, whilst a complaint to the department may be dealt with lower down and never reach him.

Sometimes Parliament can press home upon Ministers a case of importance, as over Crichel Down in July 1954. Sir Thomas Dugdale, Minister of Agriculture, admitted maladministration by some of his officials, of which he had been unaware. He accepted Ministerial responsibility and announced his resignation. It is doubtful whether, in modern circumstances, this is necessary over decisions about which the Minister could not possibly be informed. The doctrine of Ministerial responsibility is met if it has enabled Parliament to raise a particular matter and if—as Sir Thomas Dugdale had done—the Minister takes the earliest steps to correct an abuse of power or an error of judgment.

The appointment in April 1967 of the Parliamentary Commissioner for Administration was a further instance of the co-operation of Cabinet and Parliament in the political control of the executive. The Bill became law because it was initiated by the Cabinet and given a place in its legislative programme. At the same time the creation of this new office extended the range of parliamentary inquiry into the actions of Ministers and departments.

This extension was only possible because the Parliamentary Commissioner could be empowered to do things that could not be allowed to a Member of Parliament—an illustration of the limited capacity of Parliament to control the executive. The Parliamentary Commissioner could be activated only by an M.P. and was supervised by a select committee of the House: but his effectiveness depended upon powers of access to confidential and secret departmental papers and files that an M.P. could not be granted.

It is too early to say how effective will be the work of the Parliamentary Commissioner. From April to December 1967 he investigated 188 cases, in only nineteen of which he found 'some elements of maladministration'.[24] The Select Committee on the Parliamentary Commissioner reported that 'for the most part the administrative defects actually found ... have so far been relatively trivial in relation to the types of maladministration described in the House and elsewhere as the likely subject matter of investigations by a Parliamentary Commissioner.'[25]

The 'relatively trivial' defects so far found may in part be due to the limits on the jurisdiction of the Parliamentary Commissioner. In November 1968 he announced that he would extend his inquiries into the nature and not only the form of departmental decisions.[26] But another and more important reason may be the high standard of civil service administration.

One hidden effect of the appointment of the Parliamentary Commissioner was that Ministers and their departments, in arriving at decisions, began to be continuously conscious of the possibility of a reference to him.

The most important case of maladministration found by the Parliamentary Commissioner was in December 1967 when he recommended the reversal of the refusal by two Foreign Secretaries to pay compensation to survivors of Sachsenhausen concentration camp. The Cabinet's acceptance of his recommendation was announced to Parliament in February 1968.

The nature of the executive in a system in which the Cabinet forms part of Parliament is complex.

The Cabinet has a dual role. It appears in Parliament as the chief decision-making organ in the State, responsible for all that is done by Ministers and civil servants: and is thus answerable as the Executive to the Legislature. At the same time the Cabinet acts as part of Parliament and on its behalf in helping to subject the actions of civil servants to political control.

But for this second role of the Cabinet, continuous political control of the decision-making process could not be made effective.

(3) Crown and Cabinet

By the 1950s and 1960s it was possible to analyse and describe the Cabinet without direct reference to actions of the Sovereign.

As an integral part of the Constitution, the Crown continued to be in a general way of vital importance to Cabinet government. It helped to draw the distinction between Government and Nation, between Party and State. That each succeeding Cabinet exercised authority as 'Her Majesty's Government' made clearer the reality of politics and facilitated the rise and the maintenance of the two-party system: the majority party could exercise the full powers of the Cabinet (including royal prerogatives used on the advice of Ministers) without becoming identified with the State as such.

This royal function could be, as in Commonwealth countries, discharged by a constitutional Governor General or President: as Bagehot pointed out, an 'unroyal' Cabinet system would work.[27] But the function is better discharged by a Head of State who holds the office without question, who represents the continuity of the State and who does not have to be drawn from public life.

The role of the Crown in relation to the Cabinet depends upon the doctrine that the Monarch must act in such a way as not to get involved in party political conflict. This doctrine was defined with increasing clarity as power was transferred from Crown to Parliament, and the Cabinet came to depend for its existence upon Parliament and then the electorate.

The doctrine became established as the only basis for a constitutional monarchy when a stable mass two-party system arose. For thereafter any such involvement would lead to an attack upon the Crown by a party that felt itself discriminated against and which would sooner or later form a Government. It became clear that the practical implication of this doctrine was that the Crown should always act on the advice of Ministers: so that responsible Ministers and never the Crown could be blamed for any act done in the name of the Crown.

The first open statement of this doctrine was perhaps in 1841 when Russell had to tell Parliament that the Cabinet and the Cabinet alone was responsible for the Queen's Speech.[28] This was done not to assert the rights of the Cabinet, but to protect Queen Victoria from possible misunderstanding.

Bagehot saw that royal rights that cannot be exercised are not rights at all. He wrote that 'a Republic has insinuated itself beneath the folds of a monarchy'. But he considered that the Crown still had influence upon the Cabinet: 'It is wonderful how much a Sovereign can do.' None the less the famous rights that in his view were still held by the Crown – 'to be consulted, to encourage and to warn'[29] – do not amount to much: they are the attributes of a Head of State without powers.

That the Crown had rights to intervene in political affairs continued to be asserted and believed down to the time of King George V. This led the Crown to attempt to exercise influence in various ways: and until the 1930s or thereabouts some reference to the Crown was necessary to a description of the Cabinet.

One power that Queen Victoria exercised without challenge was that of demanding a meeting of the Cabinet to act as a kind of court of appeal against the Prime Minister or other Ministers. Between 1859–61 almost weekly Cabinets were held at the behest of the Queen.[30] This power was an extreme version of the right to seek advice: the Queen always accepted in the end the considered view of the Cabinet. After Queen Victoria this power would have been considered intolerable as being incompatible with the evolution of the Cabinet: and thus fell into desuetude.

Still in the twentieth century the right of the Crown to choose a Prime Minister was generally upheld. In times of doubt or difficulty when there was no evident Prime Minister, this was considered to be a reserve right necessary to the smooth working of the Constitution. The form of royal appointment has not been challenged; by unbroken practice a Prime Minister is appointed by a summons to the Palace and an invitation to assume the office and form a Government. This or some other formal creation of a Prime Minister is necessary: just as Ministers must be formally entrusted with the seals of office on kissing hands or by some other similar arrangement. It is an aid to the general function of the Crown as the formal embodiment of the State to go on as we do.

How far the Crown had a real as distinct from a formal power depended upon the acceptance or otherwise by Ministers of the power. In practice it is hard to find any example of the Crown actually choosing a Prime Minister from the time of Queen Victoria, who certainly thought she possessed this power. Sometimes an unwelcome Prime Minister was forced upon her by the balance of parties, as in the case of Gladstone in 1886. Even when there were minority Governments the effective decision was taken by the politicians who negotiated with one another.

The reality was for the first time indicated when Bonar Law insisted, in 1922, on being elected leader of the Conservative Party before accepting the King's invitation to become Prime Minister. This was the first occasion on which a political party openly exercised the actual power and the role of the Crown was reduced to a formality.

Despite this precedent, a Conservative leader was still held to 'emerge' — that is to say that a consensus formed in the party that a particular person should be the next leader. If such a person was to fill the office of Prime Minister he was elected leader after being invited by the Crown to form an Administration. The meeting that elected a leader usually consisted of Conservative M.P.s, peers and parliamentary candidates. Such elections were confirmatory of an emerged leader and were normally unanimous.

The Crown, therefore, continued in form to choose Conservative Prime Ministers — but in form only, because the consensus in favour of a leader was expressed by the established party leaders.

George V's choice of Baldwin over Curzon was in accord with the weight of advice given by Conservative party leaders;[31] as was the choice of Mr Macmillan over Mr Butler in January 1957. Queen Elizabeth sent for Sir Alec Douglas-Home in November 1963 on the advice of the retiring Prime Minister and asked him to see whether he could form an Administration. Ramsay MacDonald's choice in 1931 as the Prime Minister of a National Government was in effect made by leaders who together commanded a majority in the Commons.

The final and open passing of this royal power came when both parties, in a stable two-party system, elected their leaders.

The Labour Party had from the beginning elected its leaders at a meeting of the parliamentary party. Ramsay MacDonald was sent for by the King in 1924 and 1929 as the leader of the Labour Party. That the leader in office was the only person the Monarch could send for after a Labour electoral victory was finally settled inside the parliamentary party in 1945. On that occasion Laski, Morrison and others pressed Attlee not to go to the Palace before calling a meeting of the party in the new Parliament so that it could elect a leader. Attlee ignored these representations and accepted the King's invitation.[32] In 1950 there was no hint that Attlee, and in 1964 that Mr Harold Wilson, should not forthwith become Prime Minister.

On July 22nd, 1965 the Conservatives introduced a formal system of election of the leader by ballot. The election was limited, as in the Labour Party, to M.P.s. Mr Heath was the first leader to be so elected on July 28th, 1965.

Thereafter there would always be two elected party leaders and whichever won a general election would automatically be sent for by the Queen. No element of choice remained.

But what if a Prime Minister died or resigned or otherwise lost office? By definition there could not be an elected leader to take over, as there could be only one such leader of a party at a time.

In 1957 the Parliamentary Committee of the Parliamentary Labour Party (the Shadow Cabinet) laid down the procedure that the Labour Party would follow in such circumstances. In a published statement (which I drafted for the Committee) it was declared that a meeting of the parliamentary party should be held forthwith to elect a leader who alone could be entitled to accept the Monarch's invitation to become Prime Minister.

In order to ensure that the Queen's government went on smoothly, the party meeting would have to go into immediate and continuous session until a new leader was elected.

The Conservative Party has not decided how they would proceed if a Prime Minister of their party ceased to hold office. Having once taken the decisive step of electing their leader, it is inconceivable that they would revert to the 'emergence' of a leader.

Thus the power of the Crown to choose a Prime Minister became a confirmatory one: an acceptance of the choice of the parties and of the electorate.

By far the most important rights claimed for the Crown were those that would, if exercised, involve direct interference with the Cabinet or Parliament: the veto, the dissolution of Parliament, the dismissal of Ministers, the refusal of a dissolution. All these rights were asserted as late as the reign of King George V. The Parliament Act of 1911, it was argued, had altered the whole balance of the Constitution and revived powers latent in the Crown. Bonar Law, Leader of the Opposition, told the King in 1912: 'They say ... the prerogative of veto is dead. That was true as long as there was a buffer between you and the House of Commons, but they have destroyed this buffer and it is no longer true.' George V in a letter to Asquith wrote of himself being 'deprived of the assistance of the Second Chamber'. Throughout this crisis George V assumed that he had the constitutional power and right both to refuse assent to a Bill and to dismiss Ministers. In September 1913 he wrote to Asquith in regard to this latter power: 'Should the Sovereign never exercise this right?'[33]

One royal right can be dismissed straightaway – namely the right to dissolve Parliament against the advice of Ministers. It is a contradiction in terms, for the Monarch cannot legally effect a dissolution of Parliament without the co-operation of senior Ministers which, by definition, would not be forthcoming. Dissolution of Parliament necessitates an Order in Council and the Privy Council cannot be summoned without the advice of the Lord President: it requires a Proclamation under the Great Seal, which cannot be affixed save by the Lord Chancellor.[34]

The remaining rights claimed for the Crown in George V's time – veto, refusal of a dissolution, dismissal of Ministers – all boil down to the single right to dismiss Ministers: for Ministers whose advice in such matters was not taken would have no choice but to resign. This was made clear to Queen Victoria by Lord Russell in 1866: 'Your Majesty would be entirely free either to accept that advice [to dissolve Parliament] or to adopt the alternative, namely the resignation of your Majesty's Ministers.' In 1910 George V actually refused Asquith a dissolution, but gave way when the Cabinet decided to resign.[35]

In 1924 Asquith argued differently. The vote of the Liberals had led to the defeat of Ramsay MacDonald's Government but Asquith did not want a general election and maintained that the King need not accept the Prime Minister's request for a dissolution.[36] Asquith would undertake neither to form a Government himself nor to join a coalition with Baldwin. The King was reluctant but felt he had no other alternative than to accept the advice of a Prime Minister who did not command a majority in Parliament, but who could make any other feasible Government impossible.

Although no further claims of a right to dismiss Ministers were made by or on behalf of the Crown, they were asserted as late as 1959 by Sir Ivor Jennings in the third edition of his *Cabinet Government*. Not only did he maintain that 'the right to dismiss Ministers as a matter of right cannot be denied': he went further. He gave examples which, in his view, would justify the exercise of the right by the Queen. 'She would be justified in refusing to assent to a policy which subverted the democratic basis of the Constitution, by unnecessary or indefinite prolongations of the life of Parliament, by a gerrymandering of the constituencies in the interests of one party, or by fundamental modification of the electoral system to the same end.'[37]

Any act by the Crown in any of these instances would involve it in party politics. How can the Crown decide what is an 'unnecessary' prolongation of Parliament? Had the then Government decided to prolong Parliament to the end of the Japanese war, would this have been unnecessary? The Opposition would have thought so, the Government not. How can the Crown decide whether the electoral system is being 'fundamentally' modified or the constituencies gerrymandered? Did the 1885 Redistribution Act or the abolition of university seats amount to this? The Opposition thought so, the Government not.

Underlying Sir Ivor Jennings's argument is the same fallacy that underlay King George V's claims in the 1912 crisis—namely that it is the duty of a Monarch to protect the Constitution and that he can be blamed if he does so or fails to do so. In his letter of August 11th, 1913 to Asquith, about assenting or refusing to assent to the Home Rule Bill, George V wrote: 'Whatever I do I shall offend half the people.'[38] But the King should not put himself in such a position: it is for Ministers not the Crown to be blamed. It cannot be the function of the Crown to protect the Constitution. The remedy against abuse of the Constitution lies in Parliament, in disagreements within the assumed unconstitutional party, in public opinion: in a word, in the spirit and will of politicians and people. If that went, then the Constitution would already be gone.

Any attempt by the Crown to depart from the principle of accepting the advice of the Cabinet must risk involving it in a clash with the Government. As Harcourt told the King in a personal interview in 1912: If he refused assent to the Irish Home Rule Bill then, in the ensuing general election, Home Rule would not be mentioned, and the sole question would be—'Is the country governed by the King or by the people?'—and every Minister from Mr Asquith downwards would attack the King personally.[39]

Even should those who supported the King win such an election, the Crown would be inextricably involved in party politics and the other party would sooner or later win an election.

For well over a century the powers of the Crown have not been used, although they were believed by people of influence to exist.

The powers were not used because they could not be without bringing the Crown into direct conflict with the Government. Victoria never attempted to challenge the right of the Cabinet to determine policy. George V always found that the circumstances were not appropriate to the use of powers that he believed belonged to the Crown. In fact no circumstances could have been appropriate.

Even as early as the first half of the nineteenth century, although 'the Crown took up a great deal of the politicians' time ... in planning a course of action Cabinets gave far more thought to the actual complexity of the problem, to the anticipated response of foreign powers, the views of the public and the press ... to the reactions of the House of Commons, than to the royal views.'[40]

Since George V's time – and in fact a good deal earlier – the powers of the Crown to intervene have lapsed. Rights that cannot be exercised cease to be rights. All the powers of the Crown are as dead as the veto.

This is the logical conclusion of the doctrine that the Crown must not become involved in party politics.

How far the Crown can still exercise influence it is impossible to say. The effectiveness of influence is imprecise and hard to measure and it may come from more than one quarter. It is constitutionally proper for the Monarch to give advice as it is, indeed, for any interested body or parson or newspaper to advise the Cabinet how to act.

Influence that may be exercised by the Crown differs in this from influence exercised by pressure groups or newspapers: these, unlike the Sovereign, can threaten to take overt action of some kind if their advice is rejected.

On the other hand and perhaps for this very reason, or because of the Monarch's continuity of political information, his influence may be the greater. However, the exercise of influence presupposes that the Cabinet, which is the object of influence, alone decides whether or not to be influenced: it is a relationship between a Crown without political power and a Cabinet that is the seat of political authority.

Thus by the 1950s and 1960s the doctrine had been fully established that the Monarch must accept the advice of Ministers and that these and not the Crown must bear any blame that may be apportioned.

This established beyond challenge the role of the Crown as the embodiment of the State and as the best means of facilitating the working of the Constitution.

The British constitutional monarchy by remaining unquestionably above the party political battle is assured of the loyalty and affection of Parliament, political parties and people.

CHAPTER 5

ROLE OF THE PRIME MINISTER

(1) Rise of the Prime Minister

A measure of the rise in importance of the office of Prime Minister is the change that has come since Bagehot's remark made in 1867: 'If you tell a cabman to drive to "Downing Street" he most likely will never have heard of it'—an observation echoed forty years later by Margot Asquith in 1908: 'No taxi-driver knew where No. 10 was.'[1]

In early Cabinets the Prime Minister was the first among equals, and sometimes hardly that. Lord North's name always appeared very low down in the list of Ministers present at the Cabinet in the Minutes sent to the King.[2]

As a stable two-party system became established and the leader of one or other of two disciplined parties had a title to the office of Prime Minister following an electoral victory by his party—a clear trend became apparent towards the rise to pre-eminence of the Prime Minister. He became the leader and the personification of the party: he was more responsible than all the other leaders put together for the electoral fate of the party.

Powers and rights accrued to him that had not previously been possessed by Prime Ministers.

Up to the middle of the nineteenth century any Minister could convene a Cabinet. In 1778 Lord North as Prime Minister left Sandwich, the First Lord, to arrange Cabinet meetings, writing to him: 'I am at present engaged from morning till night with the House of Commons and the loan, but will attend any meetings where my presence is required.'[3]

By Aberdeen's Administration (1852–5) it had become customary for a Minister who summoned a Cabinet to mention the matter first to the Prime Minister.[4]

The sole right of the Prime Minister to call a Cabinet was established by Gladstone and Disraeli. In 1870 Gladstone told Granville that 'the Cabinet appears not to have been called in the usual manner through me': thereafter the Prime Minister's acquired right was respected. Disraeli on two occasions – over the annexation of Fiji and over the Bulgarian atrocities – simply ignored requests by some of his colleagues to hold a Cabinet. The extreme position was reached in 1894 when Gladstone went on a holiday to Biarritz and forbade any meeting of the Cabinet in his absence.[5] Today, when the Prime Minister is abroad or is ill, he puts a colleague designated by him in charge of the Cabinet. Cabinets have occasionally been held in the absence of the Prime Minister either with his knowledge or without his objection. In 1918 Lloyd George once absented himself from the Cabinet to prepare a speech for that afternoon in the House of Commons. In November 1924 the Secretariat, at the request of the Foreign Office, called a hurried Cabinet meeting of available Ministers, following the murder of Lee Stack in Egypt. At the end Austen Chamberlain telephoned Baldwin at Chequers to get his approval of the Cabinet's position, which he gave without demur.[6]

So complete became the Prime Minister's exclusive right to call or approve the calling of the Cabinet that even informal meetings of Ministers could be thought to infringe it. Around midnight on March 14th, 1968 a number of Cabinet Ministers – of which I was one – gathered in Mr George Brown's room in the House of Commons. We talked about the report on the tape that the Prime Minister and the Chancellor had been to a Privy Council at the Palace concerning an Order in Council declaring a Bank Holiday. The House was in an all-night sitting and we wondered how we should answer questions that members would be certain to put to us; so we telephoned the Prime Minister and asked to see him – to be met by the reproof that we were an 'irregularly called Cabinet'. It was to this that Mr George Brown referred in his resignation speech on March 18th, 1968 – 'my protest was

F

brushed aside on the basis that what I had done was in itself irregular.'

In fact about a dozen Ministers were in the small hours invited by the Prime Minister to the Cabinet room at No. 10.

In the matter of the appointments of Ministers, Gladstone and Disraeli followed the then established practice of consulting some of their principal colleagues beforehand on the composition of the Cabinet. In 1874 Disraeli arranged the membership of his Cabinet with Derby, Cairns, Northcote and Hardy. In 1892 Gladstone consulted with Rosebery, John Morley, Harcourt, Kimberley, Arnold Morley, Spencer and the Chief Whip, Marjoribanks. By 1902 Balfour found it possible to form a Cabinet without prior discussions: and this example was followed by Campbell-Bannerman in 1905 and by Asquith in 1908.[7] In 1924 Ramsay MacDonald had to look up in Whitaker the posts he had to fill[8] — but he filled them on his own authority — as did all subsequent Prime Ministers.

The appointment of a junior Minister was, with few exceptions, long regarded as the right of the senior Minister. Although Peel named Gladstone as Under Secretary of State for the Colonies, Gladstone himself when he was Prime Minister spoke in 1880 of junior Ministers as being 'the appointments of the Secretary of State'.

Lloyd George was the first Prime Minister to treat the making of junior Ministers as the prerogative of the Prime Minister.[9] This was, I believe, the practice of all subsequent Prime Ministers: certainly of Attlee and Mr Wilson.

Gladstone at one time (according to Harcourt) 'entertained great doubts as to the right of a Prime Minister to require a Cabinet Minister to resign. I know that he tried it in one case for convenience of recon- struction: he was point blank refused and acquiesced.'[10]

But by 1884 when Gladstone was considering the removal of a Minister, Harcourt told him: 'I confess I have never doubted that Cabinet offices were held *durante bene placito* of the Prime Minister.' By 1887 the right to dismiss was so well established that when Salisbury was reconstructing his Cabinet, after Lord Randolph Churchill's resignation,

Northcote learned only from the newspapers that he was no longer Foreign Secretary.[11]

The most ruthless exercise of the Prime Minister's now constitutional right to dismiss Ministers at his own discretion was by Mr Macmillan in July 1962. On one day he dismissed seven members of his Cabinet – the Lord Chancellor, the Chancellor of the Exchequer, the Secretary of State for Scotland, the Minister of Defence, the Minister without Portfolio, the Minister of Housing and the Minister of Education.

I understand that Eden expressed grave doubts whether this action was constitutional. In his view if there was to be such a far-reaching reconstruction of the Cabinet, there should first have been a Cabinet meeting. But, from a constitutional point of view, the right to dismiss one Minister implies the right to dismiss several at a time. None of the Ministers concerned challenged Mr Macmillan's right to dismiss him. The political wisdom of what Mr Macmillan did is another matter. (see below, p. 95).

The major right acquired by the Prime Minister – considerably later than the others – was that of advising the Crown on his own authority to dissolve Parliament. The implicit or open threat to use this power became the most potent instrument in his hand for maintaining discipline in his parliamentary party.

For a long time it was the Cabinet and not the Prime Minister that settled this matter and sometimes the Prime Minister's views were rejected by the Cabinet.

When Lord Melbourne wanted to resign in 1841 the Cabinet decided on a dissolution. In 1868 some Ministers were very angry because Disraeli asked for a dissolution without calling a Cabinet. In 1878 the Cabinet debated for three hours whether or not to have a general election after the Congress of Berlin. Gladstone in 1894 wanted to dissolve but could not carry his Cabinet. In 1895, following the defeat of Lord Rosebery's Government, there was prolonged debate in the Cabinet before the decision to dissolve was reached. In 1905 Balfour wanted to go to the country but the Cabinet insisted on resignation.[12]

Asquith laid down the general proposition: 'Such a question as the dissolution of Parliament is always submitted to the Cabinet for ultimate decision.' Both the 1910 dissolutions were discussed in the Cabinet.[13]

This was the accepted doctrine down to the first world war. Within a few years it had radically changed. In 1916 when Asquith resigned, the King anticipated that if Bonar Law accepted an invitation to form a Government he might make the condition that a dissolution be granted. The King consulted Haldane who advised: 'The only Minister who can properly give advice as to a dissolution of Parliament is the Prime Minister.'[14] When Lloyd George was considering a dissolution in 1918 there was no question of consulting the Cabinet as a whole. Balfour agreed with Bonar Law that 'the responsibility of a dissolution must rest with the Prime Minister'.[15]

News of a possible dissolution leaked out and the matter was raised in Parliament in November 1918. Balfour told the House: 'There is no custom more clearly defined than that what advice on this matter should be given to the Sovereign is a question not for the Cabinet but for the Prime Minister.' He brushed aside an intervention by Mr Dillon, who correctly stated that 'the custom has always been that the advice should be given with the consent of the Cabinet'.[16] Thus in four years or so a new doctrine of great importance to constitutional practice was established.

In 1923 Baldwin consulted four Ministers about a dissolution. All advised delay but 'in great deference, recognizing that fixing these matters is your special perquisite'. Baldwin decided on an election.[17]

From 1841 down to the first world war, every resignation of a Government, every dissolution of Parliament was discussed and decided in the Cabinet. Thereafter these matters were always determined by the Prime Minister on his own authority. To this there was only one exception when the Labour Cabinet in 1924 'after a stormy debate' decided to go to the country.[18]

A discussion, so brief as not to constitute an exception, took place in 1950 in the Cabinet about the consequences of a possible defeat in Parliament. I give more details of this in Chapter 9.

I had some foreknowledge of Attlee's decision to dissolve in 1951. He told me of his intention because I was due to go to a conference at

Victoria Falls and he wished me to give prior warning to Sir Godfrey Huggins, Prime Minister of Southern Rhodesia, that the announcement of an election would come in the middle of the conference. I begged Attlee to reconsider his decision to dissolve, but he laconically replied that he had made up his mind. In the event the general election was announced some days earlier than was intended because it became known that the *Daily Mirror* was about to come out with the correct date. The Cabinet was certainly not consulted. Herbert Morrison, who was in Canada, was informed only shortly before the announcement was made and disagreed with the timing. Mr Harold Wilson, following the practice of his predecessors, made up his own mind in 1966 without consulting the Cabinet.

A number of other factors enhanced the status of the Prime Minister. He had influence over the composition of the Cabinet agenda and the order of items (but see Chapter 7, p. 112). He could probably postpone a matter under discussion if he felt it was going the wrong way: though a similar proposal could be made by any other Minister. With the coming of radio and television the more frequent appearances of the Prime Minister raised him further above his colleagues. He could, if he wished, reduce the number of critics or Ministers of independent mind and increase the number of loyal supporters in the Cabinet.

The main intangible source of the Prime Minister's special position was the increasing feeling amongst other Ministers in the Cabinet that they needed a leader possessed of special authority. The senior members of Campbell-Bannerman's Cabinet found it very difficult to carry on while the Prime Minister was ill and his office virtually in commission in early 1908.[19] Similarly Attlee's illness in 1951 made it the more difficult for the Cabinet to handle the crisis of Bevan's resignation.

A Prime Minister who was a first among equals no longer corresponded to the needs of Cabinet government.

(2) Prime Ministerial Government?

Mr Crossman amongst others has argued that so great was the concentration of power in the Prime Minister that he in effect displaced the

Cabinet. The 'point of decision' passed upward to the Prime Minister: the reality of the Constitution was now that Cabinet government had given way to Prime Ministerial government.[20]

Similar views have sometimes been voiced by resigning Ministers. In March 1922 E. S. Montagu, Secretary of State for India, who resigned when an action of his was disowned by the Cabinet, said in the House that under Lloyd George there had been 'the total, complete, absolute disappearance of the doctrine of Cabinet responsibility'.[21]

Mr George Brown in his letter to the Prime Minister on leaving the Cabinet gave as his main motive 'the way this Government is run and the manner in which we reach our decisions' (*The Times*, March 16th, 1968). In his resignation speech in the House two days later, he elaborated this point. After speaking of the gravity of the situation, he went on: 'It is in just such a situation that it is essential for Cabinet government to be maintained ... Equally it is in just such a situation that temptation to depart from it is at its greatest. Power can very easily pass not merely from Cabinet to one or two Ministers but effectively to sources quite outside the political control altogether.'

Mr Crossman's argument rests on two main points: first that the Prime Minister's control over the party machine inside and outside Parliament has raised him to unassailable supremacy; secondly, that Attlee decided to make the atom bomb and Eden to invade Suez without consulting the Cabinet.

Before going into the merits of these points, we should note that neither of them is as novel nor as significant as is sometimes made out. 'The writers of the Prime Ministerial school ... overrate his power today and underrate the power he had in the past.'[22]

As we have seen, the Prime Minister's position as party leader was an important factor in the rise of his status and powers. But Prime Ministers dominated the political scene before Attlee and Eden. As early as 1882 *The Times* wrote of Gladstone that 'in the eyes of the Opposition as indeed of the country he is the Government and he is the Liberal Party';[23] and on another occasion that it was only occasionally, at official banquets, that the public was reminded that the Cabinet contained other members, besides the Prime Minister.[24] Writing of this same period, A. J. Balfour said: 'Gladstone *was* the Opposition. It was he who scattered Disraeli's majority: and he did it alone.'[25]

The high point in the rise in the power and status of the Prime Minister came with Lloyd George. He himself saw foreign ambassadors, sometimes without notifying the Foreign Secretary. He in effect put the Cabinet into suspension during most of 1919 whilst he was negotiating at Versailles. Lloyd George came nearest to 'becoming an extra-parliamentary governor like the President of the United States'.[26] So far from there being a steady ascent in the powers of the Prime Minister, a decline occurred after Lloyd George.

Regarding the second point, that Attlee and Eden took major decisions without consulting the Cabinet—here, too, decisions of importance had previously been made by Prime Ministers outside the Cabinet.

In 1797, in order to conceal the details of the negotiations with France, Malmesbury actually wrote false or 'ostensible' dispatches which could be circulated to Ministers and another set 'which must ... be entirely suppressed' and were seen only by Grenville and Pitt. Castlereagh in 1815 signed a secret treaty of alliance with Austria and France without the Cabinet's knowledge and contrary to its instructions at the time.[27]

In 1897 the decision to reinforce the troops at the Cape—a critical step towards war—was taken by Lord Salisbury, the Prime Minister, on the advice of the Colonial Secretary, Joseph Chamberlain.[28]

In the autumn of 1924 the Prime Minister and the Chancellor of the Exchequer alone authorized the publication of an agreement with the Soviet Union for a treaty and a loan about which the Cabinet knew nothing.[29]

In April 1938 Chamberlain and Halifax determined the British response to the German seizure of Austria; and these two agreed to naval staff talks with the French. In September 1938 Chamberlain sent a telegram to Hitler to arrange a meeting and later signed the Munich declaration before informing the Cabinet.[30]

All these cases were subsequently referred to the Cabinet: but the acts were done. As Haldane said of the 1924 Russian treaty and loan, the

Cabinet could not go back on the decision 'without shaking the Ministry to its foundations'.[31]

These examples are in one respect more striking than those of Attlee and Eden for they were taken either by the Prime Minister alone or in concert with one or two colleagues. Attlee and Eden acted in agreement with a significant number of their senior colleagues who together had great influence in the Cabinet.

The question of Attlee's responsibility for the decision on the atom bomb and of Eden's for the decision on Suez involves consideration of the 'partial Cabinet'.

I use this term to denote a number of Ministers who constitute part only of the Cabinet but act for a time as if they were the Cabinet.

A partial Cabinet is different from an inner Cabinet in that it is an organized part of the Cabinet system. Typically a partial Cabinet is a standing or ad hoc committee presided over by the Prime Minister, which may – in matters of great moment and secrecy – prepare policies in detail and sometimes take decisions without prior consultation with the Cabinet as a whole. The Cabinet is in due course informed and consulted.

The partial Cabinet depends upon a distinction among members of the Cabinet that is analogous to the arrangements for the distribution of Foreign Office telegrams. For a long time these have necessarily been sent to Ministers on a selective basis: some may be seen only by the Prime Minister and the Foreign Secretary. Salisbury marked on the cover of telegrams the names of Ministers who were to see them.[32] In 1921 some Ministers protested in Cabinet that they had not seen certain telegrams.[33] Today there are distribution lists that vary according to the type of telegram. I have known occasions in Cabinet when members have asked to see telegrams that were mentioned in the discussion but had not reached them. On the other hand I have known Cabinet Ministers who regarded their departmental duties as so heavy that they refused to look at the telegrams that were sent to their private offices. As early as 1884 Dilke protested that his inclusion on the list of recipients of telegrams involved him in too much work.[34]

A very striking step in the direction of a partial Cabinet occurred before the first world war. In January 1906 the Foreign Secretary, Sir Edward Grey, agreed with Cambon that talks should be held between the British and French staffs. At these talks plans were made for shipping British troops to France in the event of a German attack on France. Grey told the Prime Minister, Campbell-Bannerman, and Haldane, but the Cabinet was not informed nor consulted. Grey did not tell the new Prime Minister, Asquith, until 1911 that talks between the staffs had been authorized in 1906, that they had since continued and had been considered by the Committee of Imperial Defence. Later that year Lloyd George and Winston Churchill attended the Committee of Imperial Defence and discovered about the plans; perhaps through them, Morley and other members of the Cabinet became informed. In September and October 1911 there was heavy argument in the Cabinet. It was agreed that no communications should take place between the staffs which could commit the country to military intervention: and that such communications must have the previous approval of the Cabinet. Future consultations with France were debated and agreed in the Cabinet.

From 1906–11 vital decisions had been taken by about four Ministers in the Committee of Imperial Defence. Grey and Campbell-Bannerman 'gave a slant or emphasis to British foreign policy which they concealed from the Cabinet'.[35]

The cases of Attlee and Eden were not therefore startling departures: they fit into a pattern that started earlier and continued later.

I myself knew about the decision to make the atom bomb. The use of the Woomera range in Australia was involved and as Commonwealth Secretary I was a member of the Cabinet Committee dealing with the matter. We were making decisions that were continuous, highly technical and which related to military and scientific secrets of other countries besides our own. There was no question of the Prime Minister alone making decisions. A number of senior Ministers shared in every decision. When the Minutes of the committee came before the Cabinet, the Prime Minister (as Mr Crossman puts it) 'did not feel it necessary to call attention to this item'.[36] Why should he? The Minutes had been circulated to Cabinet Ministers, any one of whom could have raised the matter. Ministers receive many such papers on items in the Cabinet agenda. Owing to the composition of the Cabinet Committee there can be little doubt, had the matter been raised, that the outcome would have been no different.

The day after Nasser seized the Suez Canal a Cabinet Committee of seven was set up on July 27th, 1956. This committee supervised detailed negotiations in the complex and rapidly changing developments of the next few months, which were also holiday months. The Prime Minister and the Foreign Secretary handled the details of Anglo-French military preparations. The Cabinet met on September 11th. On October 18th, the Cabinet was informed of the plan for the invasion of the Canal area. The Cabinet Committee drafted an ultimatum to Israel and Egypt. In meetings on October 24th and 25th the Cabinet made the final decisions and approved the terms of the ultimatum. At this meeting one Minister is said to have complained of the shortage of time for making decisions. But no Cabinet Minister resigned.[37]

The same basic procedure continued under Mr Harold Wilson. The Overseas Policy and Defence Committee on a number of occasions worked out policies in detail before they came to the Cabinet—for instance proposals for defence economies and policy in Aden and elsewhere. Sanctions and the conduct of negotiations were supervised by the Rhodesia Committee. Final decisions were made by the Cabinet.

Thus the two concrete examples cited as proof of Prime Ministerial government (and other later examples that could be prayed in aid) turn out to be instances of partial Cabinets—which is something wholly different; for in a partial Cabinet a Prime Minister cannot act independently and in virtue of his office.

A partial Cabinet contains influential members of the Cabinet who can be said to represent it in the sense that collectively they carry very great influence within it. These members must be unanimous or nearly so before a partial Cabinet can function as such: otherwise there would be no certainty, and indeed little hope, of carrying the Cabinet. Dissenting Ministers might well insist on taking the issue straight to the

Cabinet. In a partial Cabinet the Prime Minister's views might be rejected. Where there have been protests in the Cabinet against a partial Cabinet, these have been in reality directed against a particular policy rather than against the method by which it has been reached: this was so in 1911 and over Duff Cooper's resignation in 1938.

A partial Cabinet is the very opposite of Prime Ministerial government: it presupposes that the Prime Minister carries influential Cabinet colleagues with him, and that these will, with the Prime Minister, convince the Cabinet if policy is questioned when the Cabinet is informed. In fact Cabinets of all parties have accepted partial Cabinets as necessary, in proper circumstances, to the conduct of the affairs of the State: just as they accept, for the same reason, the selective distribution of telegrams.

Partial Cabinets, but not Prime Ministerial government, have become an accepted and established part of the Cabinet system.

(3) Checks on the Prime Minister

Despite the rise of the Prime Minister there are restraints upon him that make Prime Ministerial government impossible.

Prime Ministers have on a fair number of occasions been overruled by their Cabinets both before and since the ascent of the Prime Minister to pre-eminence.

In 1863 the Prime Minister (Palmerston) together with the Foreign Secretary (Russell) and the Chancellor of the Exchequer (Gladstone) were overruled in their desire to recognize the Southern States in the American civil war. In the same year Palmerston tried to commit the Cabinet on another grave issue by announcing without consulting it that: 'If war broke out over Schleswig-Holstein it would not be Denmark alone with whom the aggressor would have to deal.' But when, a year later, Prussia invaded Schleswig-Holstein, Palmerston and Russell, who wanted even unilateral British intervention, were overruled by the Cabinet.[38]

In 1870 Gladstone and the Ministers who supported him failed to secure the immediate release of the Fenian prisoners. Their desire to remonstrate with Germany over the annexation of Alsace-Lorraine was prevented. In the 1880 Ministry, at the height of his influence in Parliament and country, Gladstone was overruled over sending Zebehr to help Gordon. Chamberlain's scheme for Irish Councils was turned down against Gladstone's advice. In 1889 Salisbury's Cabinet refused to accept his policy of threatening action against the Greeks in Crete. In 1894 Gladstone was overruled by the entire Cabinet on his policy of cutting the Naval Estimates. The Cabinet was prepared to face the Prime Minister's resignation. Gladstone was replaced by Rosebery.[39]

In the plenitude of his power, Lloyd George's freedom of action was limited by his Cabinet. He himself complained that he was not able to stop the Passchendaele offensive nor dismiss Robertson because he could not have carried the Cabinet. Even after his great personal electoral victory in 1918 he 'realized that his senior colleagues in the Cabinet could not be by-passed or ignored ... there was never an attempt to deceive the Cabinet'.[40]

In January 1920, Lloyd George — although backed by his Foreign Secretary, Lord Curzon — was overruled by the Cabinet on his policy of expelling the Turks from Constantinople: he himself said he 'stood alone as pro-Greek in the Cabinet'.[41]

In 1922 occurred a case when a Minister acted without Cabinet approval and then carried the Cabinet against the Prime Minister. Baldwin, the Chancellor of the Exchequer, in disregard of clear Cabinet instructions, accepted in Washington a settlement of the British debt to the United States and announced the terms as he stepped off the liner at Southampton. In Cabinet Bonar Law, the Prime Minister, was strongly opposed to the terms agreed. Only two Ministers supported him. He contemplated resignation but was overpersuaded.[42]

Eden and the War Cabinet overruled Churchill when they insisted upon a peaceful approach to Portugal over the occupation of the Azores.[43] In 1952 Churchill was in a minority in his Cabinet when it decided to leave the Suez base.[44]

Mr Harold Wilson and his Foreign Secretary were once overruled by the Cabinet on a matter of great importance.

Prime Ministers have been seriously challenged and even driven from office.

Gladstone in 1894 was compelled to resign by the revolt of his Cabinet.

Asquith was replaced by Lloyd George after a revolt in his Cabinet during a wartime crisis.

Lloyd George was overthrown at a time when his position appeared very strong after his personal electoral victory at the end of 1918. Bonar Law said: 'He can be Prime Minister for life if he likes.'[45]

He was powerful enough in April 1919 to rebuff a protest by no less than 370 Members of Parliament against his policy, by telling them that if their objections continued he would ask the constituencies to settle the matter.[46]

In 1922 Lloyd George was still apparently unassailable. He had behind him the established leaders of the Conservative majority party – Chamberlain, Balfour, Birkenhead, Churchill. His only opponents in the Cabinet were Baldwin and Griffith Boscawen and later Curzon who changed sides. Thus in the crisis Lloyd George's position in the Cabinet was secure. Austen Chamberlain, Lloyd George's chief supporter, had been unanimously elected leader of the Conservative Party only in March of the previous year.

When opposition to Lloyd George began to mount in the Conservative Party and particularly among the junior Ministers, he considered a dissolution of Parliament: but Chamberlain and the other Conservative leaders after much doubt decided to call a party meeting and quell the rebels before holding an election. On October 19th, 1922 at the Carlton Club Chamberlain and the other Conservative leaders were defeated by 187 votes to 87. In effect this was, and was intended to be, a defeat for Lloyd George who resigned within three hours without facing Parliament and without advising a dissolution.

In 1927–9, during Baldwin's second Administration, there was considerable talk in the party and the press about changing the leadership. Seventy Conservative M.P.s put down an amendment that was designed as a vote of censure on the Prime Minister.

In effect Ramsay MacDonald was overthrown by the Labour Cabinet in 1931 when he failed to carry it on a major issue. His position as Labour Prime Minister became impossible and he resigned as such. That he went on as Prime Minister of a National Government was a different matter.

In May 1940 Neville Chamberlain was forced to resign after a division in the House in which forty-one of his Conservative supporters voted against him and some sixty abstained. Chamberlain's majority was still eighty-one and in normal times this would probably have been enough to keep him in office. But this was a wartime crisis when national unity was necessary: a Prime Minister was called for, whom Labour would support. So, without any party meetings, Churchill replaced Chamberlain.

It is very doubtful whether Churchill could have postponed his retirement beyond 1955. His Cabinet, which knew the state of his health, was very restless. It is doubtful, too, whether Sir Anthony Eden could long have survived the Suez fiasco even if his health had held out.

Mr Macmillan was under such severe attack from within his own party in 1963 that it must at least be open to doubt whether he could have long remained in office had he not resigned through illness in the autumn.

Just as intangible factors enhanced the status of the Prime Minister, so they imposed a check upon him. The increased exposure of a modern Prime Minister on radio and television, which greatly raises his power when things are going well, may rapidly undermine his prestige when things are going badly. Indeed the mere passage of time may weaken his position through the overfamiliarity of the public with his manner and style of address. It may well be that the mass media of communication, which have helped to raise the Prime Minister to greater heights than his earlier predecessors, may also have shortened his political life in comparison with them.

Some light is thrown upon the status of a Prime Minister by the attempts, successful and unsuccessful, that have been made to remove a party leader who has been Prime Minister. Such men are, to a greater degree than Leaders of the Opposition who have not served in that office, in charge of the party inside and outside Parliament.

After the Conservative defeat in 1929 a determined effort was made to remove Baldwin, who had twice been Prime Minister and was soon to be the architect of a Conservative-dominated National Government.

In the autumn of 1930 demands arose amongst Conservative M.P.s for a special meeting to consider the question of the party leadership. Such a meeting was held on October 30th. It was, according to the then Conservative custom, composed of Members of Parliament, peers and parliamentary candidates. Colonel Gretton, M.P., moved a resolution, which was seconded by another M.P., that a change in the leadership of the party was necessary in the national interest. After debate it was defeated by 462 votes to 116.[47]

Sir Alec Douglas-Home was actually induced to resign by sustained opposition in his party in July 1965 – a year and a half after he had been unanimously elected leader of the party and nine months after being Prime Minister.

Although by the 1950s and 1960s the office of the Prime Minister had risen greatly in status, although the Prime Minister had acquired an authority different in kind from that of his colleagues, he was still not independent of the Cabinet. The Cabinet remained the sole source of political authority. On occasion and for a while a partial Cabinet could act in its name: but the power of a partial Cabinet always depended upon the assurance that a sufficient number of leading Ministers shared in its decisions to secure the full authority of the Cabinet in the end.

A strong Prime Minister can be very strong. He can sometimes commit the Cabinet by acts or words. But he cannot *habitually* or often do so.

A Prime Minister who habitually ignored the Cabinet, who behaved as if Prime Ministerial government were a reality – such a Prime Minister could rapidly come to grief. He would be challenged by his colleagues in the Cabinet and on occasion overridden. Theoretically a Prime Minister could dismiss all his Ministers; but then he would present his critics in the party with potent leadership: Mr Macmillan's mass dismissals in 1962 were generally held to have weakened him. Macmillan was less dominant in his new Cabinet than in his old.

Future Prime Ministers may well, like Mr Harold Wilson, regard Mr Macmillan's 'slaughter' as an example to be eschewed.[48]

A Prime Minister could not, and never does, behave as if he could govern on his own—because this would undermine his position. The attempt would be self-defeating: the Prime Minister would have less power than before he started to embark on Prime Ministerial government. He would be exchanging very real, very important and very distinctive powers for a mirage. Prime Ministers know this, whatever commentators may write—so Prime Ministerial government remains a matter of words on paper.

The truth is that the Cabinet and the party inside and outside Parliament do indeed find the Prime Minister an indispensable asset and that this gives him eminent power. But equally the Prime Minister cannot dispense with party, Parliament and Cabinet.

Occasionally a great matter of policy may be dealt with by a partial Cabinet: but the normal, regular and natural procedure is for the Cabinet to discuss and decide all great issues and emergencies—such as the application to join the Common Market; the sale of arms to South Africa; the Arab-Israeli war; the Russian occupation of Czechoslovakia.

On all such matters the Prime Minister's views will carry great weight with the members of the Cabinet; but he cannot, like an American President, ignore their views. A striking example of the difference between a British Prime Minister and an American President occurred in August 1941 during the discussions between Churchill and Roosevelt in Newfoundland over the Atlantic Charter. Roosevelt, as President, could sign on his own authority; but Churchill felt obliged to refer the matter back to the Cabinet in London.[49] Unlike a President, a Prime Minister can on occasion be overruled by his Cabinet.

The Prime Minister can exercise his greatly enhanced powers only if he carries his Cabinet with him.

PART THREE

Cabinet in Action

CHAPTER 6

CABINET IN SESSION

(1) Assembly of the Cabinet

The Cabinet can meet anywhere, on any day, at any hour.

In the eighteenth century it usually met in a private house, often that of the member who called the Cabinet together; until somewhat later it might meet in the house of a member who was sick.

From the early nineteenth century the normal meeting place was the Cabinet room in the Foreign Office: members sat in fixed places in chairs set about a room which contained a small round table. In 1856 meetings were transferred to No. 10, Downing Street, where Ministers sat around an oblong table. Down to the 1870s a Cabinet dinner was held every Wednesday, each member taking it in turn to act as host;[1] these dinners 'led to leakages by waiters and more than usual confusion as to what, if anything, had been decided'.[2]

On one occasion—February 1st, 1882—the Cabinet met in the Speaker's room in the House of Commons. This was the night before Speaker Brand moved the closure from the Chair on his own authority to bring to an end a debate that had been prolonged by Irish obstruction to forty-one and a half hours. Whilst the Cabinet discussed what proposals it would make to the House the next day, the Speaker was in the Chair.[3]

In Gladstone's last Ministry, owing to his deafness, Cabinet meetings were moved upstairs to the Picture Room at No. 10 where the Prime Minister could sit on a chair in the centre so that members could make themselves understood to him: when Rosebery took over from Gladstone in 1894, meetings were resumed in the Cabinet room.

In Lloyd George's time the Cabinet met in a number of different places. Twice in April 1920 it assembled in the dining-room at No. 10

because advantage was being taken of the Prime Minister's absence abroad to clean the Cabinet room. On May 12th, 1921 it was called in Chamberlain's room in the House of Commons (during the Prime Minister's absence abroad). In September 1921 Lloyd George summoned a Cabinet in Inverness Town Hall to suit his own convenience while on holiday. Chamberlain described this as 'outrageous' and Ministers were generally annoyed: later Sir E. Grigg expressed the view that, in regard to the erosion of Lloyd George's position, 'the rot had spread ever since he had made them dance attendance on him at Inverness.' In the same month, again during Lloyd George's absence from London, the Cabinet was called in Chamberlain's room in the House of Commons.

At Curzon's request the Cabinet met in November 1921 in his room at the Foreign Office. This was to enable it to decide whether or not to remove the cartoons by Goetz that had, much to Curzon's annoyance, been put up in the Foreign Office by the Ministry of Works. This was one occasion on which Lloyd George took a vote: it was almost unanimously against Curzon.[4]

Cabinets have for long met from time to time in the Palace of Westminster: down to about 1885 these were sometimes called 'informal' or 'quasi' Cabinets to distinguish them from those more regularly called at No. 10.[5] Today meetings are called in the Prime Minister's room in the House of Commons whenever convenient – for example to enable a particular member to take part in a debate or to allow the members to vote in an important division. Sometimes meetings are held at Chequers, usually when a full day's discussion of some subject is desired.

In important matters Mr Harold Wilson preferred Cabinet meetings at No. 10, Downing Street. This may have been because his press office can work more smoothly from there and the political correspondents can more easily gather for briefing. In 1967 a series of Cabinet meetings on entry into the Common Market culminated in a day-long meeting at Chequers at which every member spoke, heads were counted and a decision made in effect to apply for admission into the Common Market. Although this was a Cabinet meeting and minuted as such, the

Prime Minister adjourned the meeting and recalled the Cabinet a few days later at No. 10 to reach and register a formal decision.

Through most of the nineteenth century the normal day of meeting was Saturday. With the coming of the week-end habit at the turn of the century, Wednesday became the regular day with Monday kept for extra meetings if needed.[6] Attlee's Cabinets generally met on Mondays and sometimes on Thursdays as well. Under Conservative Prime Ministers the regular days were Tuesdays and Thursdays. Mr Harold Wilson had as a rule one Cabinet a week, usually on Thursdays, sometimes on Tuesdays: but a considerable number of further meetings was held. Sometimes these came with great frequency when a critical issue arose – such as the sale of arms to South Africa or the threat of war between Egypt and Israel. Alongside normal meetings, a series of Cabinets was sometimes devoted to a particular issue with no other business on the agenda: examples were a succession of Cabinets on the question of Britain's application to join the Common Market: and on the economies in public expenditure in January 1968. This useful practice was, I think, an innovation by Mr Harold Wilson.

Wherever and whenever it may meet, what constitutes a Cabinet is a summons by the Prime Minister that is transmitted to all the members. The rule is that the agenda and other papers must be distributed at least forty-eight hours before a meeting. Sometimes they arrive later than this and a Minister may have to sit up to study them in addition to the departmental papers that he habitually takes home with him.

The Cabinet can at need be summoned very quickly. A Cabinet Minister must keep his Private Office informed of his movements day and night so that he can be reached in a hurry. On occasion he may be brought from the theatre; or his car may be stopped by the police with a message that he is urgently needed for a sudden Cabinet meeting; or he may be raised from his bed, as happened to a number of members in August 1941, when the Cabinet was called at one forty-five a.m. in order to send Sir Winston Churchill in Newfoundland comments on the draft Atlantic Charter in time for his meeting next morning with President Roosevelt.[7]

Not long before midnight on March 14th, 1968 the Prime Minister, at very short notice, decided to proclaim a Bank Holiday and arranged with the Queen for a Privy Council. At the same time he caused a summons to be sent out for a Cabinet at ten a.m. the next morning, a Friday. A fully attended Cabinet thus assembled with about ten hours' notice—most of them hours of darkness.

In emergencies—as on this occasion—the business before the Cabinet may have to be raised orally: if there are papers, these may have to be read in the Cabinet room before the discussion begins.

A call to the Cabinet takes precedence over everything save a summons to the Privy Council. Ministers sometimes leave a Cabinet early to attend a Privy Council.

There is no quorum for a Cabinet. If a Minister is absent through illness or travel abroad his views are left out of account, even though he may occasionally have given his opinion to the Prime Minister who may convey it to the Cabinet. If heads are counted, absent heads are not reckoned. If some Minister is away whose presence is specially desirable for an item of business, the Prime Minister may postpone it until his return. An absent Minister may be represented by a junior Minister; but he would be entitled to speak only on specific departmental matters.

Wherever the Cabinet meets, the way it gathers and proceeds is the same.

If it is meeting at No. 10, Downing Street, members assemble a few minutes before the time set, in the antechamber outside the Cabinet room—in their hands their red, black or brown leather boxes containing their Cabinet papers. At one end of this antechamber stands a bare round table with a black oilcloth cover, a sofa and half a dozen chairs. A door gives on to a small room that used to be a waiting room for important visitors to the Prime Minister. Mr Harold Wilson converted it into an office for his political secretary. Round the walls are hat and coat pegs with the names of Ministerial offices underneath written in gothic script. At some time, presumably, these were in order of seniority: but for many years they have not been altered and some even enshrine the names of offices whose holders are not in the Cabinet.

Since there is little room to sit, most Ministers stand. They chat with one another about business or personal affairs, using first names. Officials of the Cabinet Secretariat keep a tally of Ministers as they make their appearance. Mr Attlee himself used to open the double doors that separate the antechamber from the Cabinet room. In Mr Harold Wilson's time this was usually done by a uniformed attendant.

Members then move into the Cabinet room and take their places around the table which is covered with a green baize cloth. This table was always oblong until Mr Macmillan introduced a coffin-shaped table (*see below*) which had the advantage that members could see each other better; but, on the other hand, held fewer people. Mr Harold Wilson reverted to the traditional oblong table that he had known in Attlee's Cabinet and which has room for a few over twenty people.

When they have sat down, the members take out of their boxes their folders of Cabinet papers; these folders are by tradition bright red.

The Prime Minister always sits in a chair in the middle of one of the long sides of the table with his back to the fireplace, over which hangs a picture of Walpole, and facing windows that give on to the garden and Horse Guards Parade. In the left-hand corner from the Prime Minister is a french window with steps down to the garden. This and other windows in the same wall afford a view of St James's Park. There are two clocks, one on the wall facing the Prime Minister and one on the mantelshelf behind him. Every member can see the time from his seat.

Some places at the Cabinet table are now fixed by convention. To the Prime Minister's left sits the Chancellor of the Exchequer and, beyond him, the Lord President, who is normally Leader of the House. On the Prime Minister's right is the Cabinet Secretary. His Deputy Secretary and Under Secretary sit at the narrow end of the table on the Prime

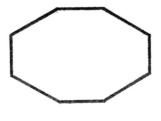

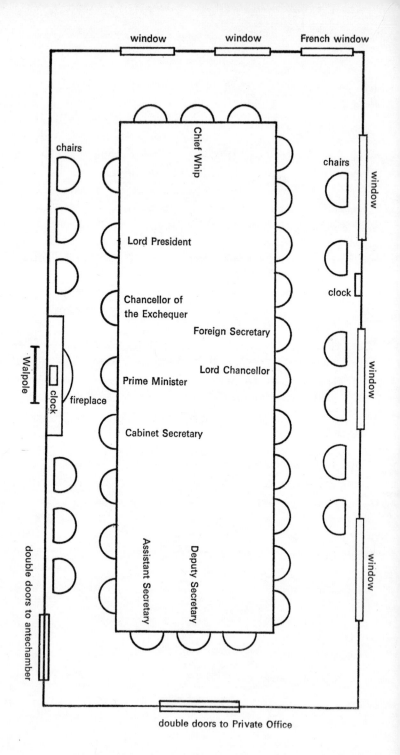

Minister's right: behind them are the double doors leading to the Private Office.

Opposite the Prime Minister, in Attlee's Cabinet, sat the Foreign Secretary: but Mr Harold Wilson has the Lord Chancellor opposite him, and on his right hand the Foreign Secretary. Another change from Attlee's time concerns the Chief Whip. He used to be called in only for the item of 'Parliamentary Business'.[8] Churchill introduced the practice by which the Chief Whip, though still not a member of the Cabinet, became a constant attender — that is to say, his name invariably appeared on the agenda as 'invited to attend'. This practice is followed by Mr Harold Wilson and the Chief Whip is present throughout the meeting. He sits in the middle of the narrow end of the table to the left of the Prime Minister. His presence is a convenience, as estimates of probable party reactions may be relevant to any item of business. Since he is not a member of the Cabinet, he can (as it is put) 'speak only when spoken to' — that is to say, only if the Prime Minister calls him. On one occasion when the Prime Minister called the Chief Whip on the merits of a matter (as distinct from the probable attitude of the party), a Minister objected on the ground that the Chief Whip was not a member of the Cabinet. The Prime Minister did not persist in his invitation to him to speak.

No other places are prescriptive to any particular office. In the past Prime Ministers decided table placings. Salisbury was careful to make arrangements upon the idea of the 'usefulness of certain contiguities'.[9]

Today seating is arranged by the Cabinet Secretary, for all I know after a word with the Prime Minister. No order of precedence is followed. There are no place-cards on the table. At the first meeting of a Cabinet the Secretary, with a seating plan in his hand, shows members where to sit. When a new member enters the Cabinet, his place is likewise indicated to him.

Occasionally a member may change his seat. When Derby withdrew his resignation in 1878 he moved away from his seat next to Disraeli. I once moved after asking the Cabinet Secretary to put me further from Hugh Dalton, who kept up a running commentary on the proceedings. On the whole the best places are on the long side of the table opposite the Prime Minister, as it is somewhat easier from here to catch his eye.

There are chairs against the wall in case more people are present than can be accommodated at the table.

On the Cabinet table are stacks of No. 10 writing paper and envelopes; red and blue and ordinary pencils; cut-glass carafes of water and tumblers—never enough of these to go round: one member often asks another to pass him a carafe or a glass. The hard biscuits, which were still there in Asquith's day and which he says were believed to date from Pitt's time, have disappeared. Asquith also reports that there was a taboo on smoking. In Lloyd George's time this strictness began to be somewhat relaxed. In meetings of Ministers, as distinct from Cabinets, smoking was allowed: as it also began to be in Cabinets held in the House of Commons. In 1922 Chamberlain, who was presiding, gave permission to smoke during a suspension of the Cabinet to await a Minister who had been summoned. The ban was lifted by the first Labour Government in 1924.[10] It was reimposed by Attlee—as part of a campaign to reduce smoking in order to save dollars and help the balance of payments. Sir Winston Churchill reintroduced smoking in 1951: it has been allowed in all subsequent Cabinets.

(2) Atmosphere of the Cabinet

From the moment when members are seated and the Prime Minister has called the Cabinet to order members refer to each other by the title of their office. The Cabinet is not just a meeting of persons, but a continuing body that has for centuries been the seat of ultimate political authority. Members address their remarks to the Prime Minister and interventions start with the words 'Prime Minister'. References to other members are usually directed through the Prime Minister and in the third person: 'The Minister of Pensions said ... ' Occasionally a direct remark may be made to another member in the second person: but the official title will still be used: 'You said, Secretary of State for Defence, that ... '

Members speak as called by the Prime Minister. The usual way of indicating a desire to speak is to say 'Prime Minister' when the previous speaker has finished—or sometimes before. If several members do this together, the Prime Minister will call one of them, saying, for instance, 'Secretary of State for Wales.' Whilst someone is speaking a member may indicate his desire to speak, perhaps by waving a pencil or slightly raising his hand. Mr Harold Wilson would often indicate by gesture the order in which he intended to call the next two or three to speak.

Speeches are brief and almost always matter of fact: though sometimes passion and even anger can enter in. In 1894 Gladstone was so angry with Harcourt for not backing him on the reduction of the Estimates that he moved his chair round and turned his back on him. I have known quick and angry exchanges, sometimes as part of a discussion, sometimes cutting into it or said quietly enough not to be generally heard. At times such as these 'You' rather than the Ministerial title tends to be used.

No one today would remotely emulate Gladstone who in 1860 spent forty-five minutes on the paper duties and in 1853 three hours explaining his budget.[11] In 1931 Lloyd George told a select committee of the House of Commons that, although a Minister explaining a budget or a Bill was allowed some latitude, 'a man who makes a five-minute speech in a Cabinet is voted a bore straightaway.'[12] This is still a fair description. Not all members speak on an issue unless it is one of major importance or the Prime Minister is counting heads. Often only two or three speak, very occasionally only the Minister who expounds his paper.

Manifestations of impatience tend to check the length of speeches on matters of secondary importance or those on which the Cabinet has clearly made up its mind; or interventions of undue length. This impatience is compounded of the desire of some Ministers to reach their own business on the agenda and of others simply to conclude the Cabinet in reasonable time. Once in Mr Harold Wilson's Cabinet, when a Minister opening a discussion was expected to speak for a long time, three or four of us at the other end of the table ran a sweepstake. Each of us wrote our estimate of the length of the speech and paid our sixpence in. In fact the speech lasted just over fourteen minutes, which gives an idea of what in a modern Cabinet is regarded as the limit of tolerable length – or perhaps beyond it.

During Gladstone's long speeches some members were reported to have fallen asleep.[13] In the Balfour Cabinet the Duke of Devonshire was often asleep.[14] I have known members nod off. In the 1870s some Ministers caught up with their correspondence in Cabinet and one wrote regularly to his wife.[15] In Mr Harold Wilson's Cabinet one Minister frequently and openly read and annotated his official papers: though he was able to make trenchant observations on matters that concerned or interested him.

Members sometimes toss notes across the table to each other or pass them from hand to hand to reach a more distant Minister. Notes are usually folded double, addressed on the outside to the Minister by title. The note itself will be couched in first name terms. Notes may contain a joke, a caustic comment on some member who is speaking; propose an appointment; give or seek information; ask a member to intervene in the discussion; and the like.

Ministers who are not members of the Cabinet are invited to attend when matters concerning their departments come up for discussion. This can be an arduous experience. On the agenda will appear the statement that such and such a Minister is invited to attend for such and such an item at a specified time.

Rarely the business of the Cabinet may go quicker than expected. In that case the Minister has to drop whatever he is doing and rush over in response to a telephone message. More usually the Cabinet falls behind in its programme: sometimes so much so, that it comes to an end before the Minister has been asked to come in: or he may after a lengthy wait be told to go away. He will then be summoned again for another Cabinet.

The Minister waits in the antechamber. When you are here by yourself, it is borne in upon you how cheerless it is: one of the few places more uncomfortable than the traditional dentist's waiting-room.

At last the Minister is called in. He enters a Cabinet in full swing and looks hastily around for a vacant chair. Almost before he has time to open his red folder, he is called on by the Prime Minister to speak on the paper that he has circulated; enters into the debate and when it is concluded, leaves. Sometimes he may be asked to join in a discussion that is opened by another Minister but which concerns his department. If a fair number of non-Cabinet Ministers are invited for an item, some of them may have to sit on chairs at the back. This happened during the series of meetings on the reduction of public expenditure early in 1968. All Ministers departmentally concerned — that is, practically all full Ministers — attended throughout. Every decision affected them directly or indirectly; but they could speak only on items immediately concerning them.

The Prime Minister can summon anyone to a Cabinet. I have known our High Commissioner in Canada and officials with special knowledge to be present. The only person not connected with the public service who in my experience was invited to a Cabinet was, in Attlee's time, a high representative of the oil company involved in the Persian seizure of the Abadan refinery.

The Prime Minister will open the discussion on an item on the agenda by calling on the Minister responsible for the main paper: other Ministers with papers or closely concerned with the matter will next be called: then other Ministers as they catch the Prime Minister's eye.

Sometimes the outcome of the discussion is simple: little or no difference of opinion may have emerged. The Prime Minister on such an occasion would not sum up: the conclusions in the Minutes would reproduce those put forward in the Ministerial paper.

When difference of opinion persists, the practice of Prime Ministers varies. Gladstone and other Prime Ministers were said, if they themselves had strong views on a matter that was going against them, to delay a decision. Sir Winston Churchill did so on occasion by indulging in long monologues on an earlier item.[16]

Attlee's normal practice was to sum up the general sense of a discussion. If he had taken part in it himself he often modified his own views in his summing up in the light of the trend of the discussion. If, after the summing up, any member wished to continue the discussion, Attlee would later sum up again, perhaps with a different emphasis. Silence after the Prime Minister's summing up signified the assent of the Cabinet. Undue prolongation of the discussion against a clearly preponderant view was discouraged by manifestations of impatience.

Mr Harold Wilson brought a discussion to an end in much the same way, though he was more inclined to count heads.

At the conclusion of an item of business a member may, if the outcome is very important for his department, send out a note to be conveyed to his Private Office. I did this on one or two occasions.

The time for the conclusion of a Cabinet depends partly on the amount of business to be done and in part on the habit or inclination of a Prime Minister.

Churchill was said to dislike leaving the Cabinet room before one thirty p.m. because he was used to a rather late lunch. To the frequent inconvenience of members, the Cabinet had to go on until this hour even if work in hand did not justify it. By ten minutes past one some members began silently to leave: sometimes by the end of the session 'scarcely a moiety' remained.[17]

Under Attlee, Eden and Macmillan the Cabinet went on until as much business as possible was completed: the hour at which the Cabinet ended was therefore unpredictable and members could be considerably and unexpectedly delayed for lunch engagements on Cabinet days.

Mr Harold Wilson, in order to prevent the drawing of unfair inferences by the press of disunity or splits, did not like his Cabinets to go on beyond one p.m. and sometimes hastened the closing of a meeting or postponed business to another occasion.

Members of the Cabinet are party leaders who have grown up together in the same political movement, who know one another inside out. The fate of each depends by and large upon the behaviour and loyalty of all the others.

Despite the formality of address, the sharp interchanges that sometimes occur, despite envies and rivalries — the underlying tone of the Cabinet springs from a community of party interest.

Without this the working of the Cabinet cannot be understood. Indeed, without this, the Cabinet system could hardly work at all. It enables deadlocks to be broken, compromises to be made, co-ordination of departments to be achieved.

Only in wartime can the common end of victory keep together a

Cabinet of different parties. Leading politicians know that in ordinary times there is no substitute for common party interest. It is not Britain that does not like coalitions, but the men whose job it is to run Cabinets. In a peacetime coalition the distrust would outweigh the trust, which makes the wheels of a complex and intricate Cabinet structure go round.

Cabinet Committees that are presided over by the Prime Minister normally meet at No. 10. They are a replica of the Cabinet—with agendas, papers, Conclusions and the same degree of formality. Cabinet Committees that are chaired by other Ministers meet else-where—in a room in the Cabinet Office building or at the House of Commons. Procedure is the same but for one or two minor departures. Ministers sit in places indicated by cards giving the title of their office: this, because Cabinet Committees are held in different rooms with different shaped tables. Ministers invited to attend a committee for a specified item on the agenda do not wait outside but come straight in, since there would often be no place where they could comfortably or conveniently tarry.

The Cabinet room at No. 10 serves also as the Prime Minister's office and working place. Here he reads his papers, telegrams and briefs and receives people whom he has agreed to see or summoned. The Prime Minister, at least during office hours, sits in the chair from which he presides over the Cabinet.

When a Cabinet breaks up, the Cabinet room may merge from the place of assembly of the Cabinet into the Prime Minister's working room. A Minister may ask to have a word with the Prime Minister or may have sent him a note to this effect during the meeting and received back an assenting note.

The Prime Minister may have arranged to speak with one or more Ministers and he may ask the remaining members of the Cabinet, who otherwise tend to hang about talking, to leave the room as quickly as possible.

CHAPTER 7

HOW THINGS GET TO THE CABINET

(1) Regular Items

So long as forty-eight hours' notice can be given to the members, all that is necessary for a matter to come before the Cabinet is that it should be inscribed on the agenda. This is done by the Cabinet Secretary in consultation with the Prime Minister.

The Prime Minister is the arbiter of what gets on to the Cabinet agenda. I doubt whether any Prime Minister today could play about with the agenda as Lloyd George did: 'if he wants a subject taken first the fact that it is sixth on the agenda makes no difference.'[1] But a Prime Minister can have a considerable influence in expediting or delaying the appearance of an item on the agenda; in having it placed high or low in order; or in suggesting other ways in which a particular issue might be considered and settled—for instance by discussion between one or two Ministers concerned perhaps together with himself.

These powers cannot, as some commentators maintain, be arbitrarily used nor do they give a Prime Minister a far-reaching ability to manipulate the Cabinet. The powers are rather the expression than the cause of the Prime Minister's enhanced status. The self-same pressures gave the Prime Minister his powers concerning the agenda that produced the agenda itself: only when the agenda came into existence could these Prime Ministerial powers arise. These pressures were the need to find new ways of expediting business and of preventing the Cabinet from being over-cluttered up with work.

Of course a Prime Minister can and does sometimes use his management of the agenda with political or personal considerations in mind. But he cannot carry this very far. He presides over a Cabinet structure that itself engenders items of business and demands their conclusion with appropriate dispatch. The Prime Minister cannot block matters which clearly must be decided and which important Ministers want to get settled. A Prime Minister can manipulate business through the composition of the agenda: but only as one might alter the sluices of a river whose flow goes on.

Some matters by common consent never or hardly ever come before the Cabinet—chief amongst them, questions of State security. The Prime Minister is in personal and supreme control of these: the Foreign Secretary and Home Secretary also have personal responsibilities. Unless a matter becomes public—for instance through the exposure of a secret agent or spy—issues of security are left to these Ministers. The Cabinet could insist on being kept regularly informed, but it has never done so. Ministers do not wish to be burdened with secrets that they need not know. They trust their responsible colleagues to assert the principle of political control and to exercise this control with discretion. So far as my experience goes, political and Ministerial control of security is unquestioned and effective.

One category of items that find or force their way on to the Cabinet agenda may be classified as routine, regular or recurrent.

Two items always figure at the head of the Cabinet agenda at one meeting each week: they are both followed by the words in brackets—'(to be raised orally)'.

The first is *Parliamentary Business* for the following week. The Leader of the House reads out the proposed business for each day. Normally there is not much discussion: he is the acknowledged specialist responsible for getting through the whole business of the session and timing it properly week by week. In any case, if this item is taken in the normal way on a Thursday morning, the Opposition Shadow Cabinet will know the details before the Cabinet itself. This is because the House is informed of the following week's business on Thursday afternoon after questions. In order to enable the Opposition to decide its line and choose spokesmen before this time it is always told of proposed business before the regular meeting of the Shadow Cabinet on Wednesday.

The Cabinet will consider Parliamentary Business earlier in the week if there is no Thursday Cabinet or if some item is likely to cause division amongst the members or may split the party and should therefore be discussed. Concessions to critics may be proposed and opposed: for instance, that the Government should put down a motion in the House that a White Paper should be 'noted' rather than 'approved'. A party meeting may be suggested before the Cabinet commits itself on a matter: and the item may be postponed to a later day in the week or to a subsequent week.

Usually all the Cabinet does is to pick its spokesmen for the debates in the House – almost always the Minister departmentally concerned with the business and one or other of his junior Ministers.

On more general debates that do not fall within a Minister's departmental jurisdiction (such as a debate on the adjournment or on an Opposition motion of censure) rivalry may occur between Ministers who would like to speak. Nowadays there are in every Cabinet non-departmental Ministers who cannot have many opportunities to speak in the House and who are eager to get what chances they can.

A Minister wishing to speak on such a general subject may have a preliminary word with the Prime Minister or the Leader of the House or he may ask some Minister, who is not concerned with the issue, to suggest his name. The Leader of the House may propose a Minister when announcing the item of business or leave it open. A brief discussion may ensue. If the Prime Minister makes a suggestion, that is accepted.

Should the Prime Minister himself want to speak this is normally agreed at once: though the point may be put that his participation would give too much weight to the debate or that he might, with greater advantage, speak on a later occasion.

Once in a while the parliamentary business proposed by the Leader of the House may be tentative. Which Minister speaks may depend upon whether the Opposition moves a critical amendment: or it may not yet be known what subject the Opposition has chosen for a 'supply day' — that is one which the Opposition can use as it will; or whether the Opposition will 'give up' one of its supply days so that there can be a two-day debate on some question.

Quite a lot of to-ing and fro-ing may go on between Government and Opposition on details of this kind. If matters have to be settled after the Cabinet is over, the Leader of the House will talk with the Prime Minister and inform the Ministers concerned, probably by telephone.

Occasionally the Leader of the House may give the Cabinet a forward look in order to impress upon Ministers how tight the parliamentary timetable is and that if certain Bills, White Papers and the like are not drafted in time, they may fall by the wayside.

The second matter which appears as a routine item once a week at the head of the agenda to be raised orally is *Foreign and Commonwealth Affairs*. The Foreign Secretary tells the Cabinet about things that are happening or are likely to happen and his attitude to them. He may have had a previous word with the Prime Minister about what to disclose or to keep quiet about for the moment. I myself, when I was Foreign Secretary, did this regularly with Mr Harold Wilson. My impression is that Bevin similarly talked with Attlee.

The Foreign Secretary's verbal report is usually followed by brief questions and answers. If a major matter of foreign policy arises, this will be brought before the Cabinet by the Foreign Secretary in a prepared and previously circulated paper and under a special item on the agenda.

All White Papers automatically appear on the Cabinet agenda. These will have been processed by the appropriate committee. The Prime Minister reads out the paragraph or page numbers and Ministers interrupt if they wish to raise any points. Sometimes there can be quite considerable discussion and amendments may be made. If dissent is considerable or it becomes too difficult to redraft in Cabinet, the White Paper may be remitted to the committee, despite the protest of the Minister that this will throw out his intended programme.

Once only — it was in Mr Wilson's second Administration — have I known a White Paper that did not go before a committee and which was presented in final printed form to the Cabinet. A number of Ministers wished to question important passages in it, but were unable to do so.

Certain statistical reports come regularly before the Cabinet at monthly or quarterly intervals: such as an analysis of employment and unemployment, of the balance of trade or of payments, and the like.

(2) Matters that go direct to the Cabinet

Some questions are brought straight to the Cabinet by a Minister or by the Prime Minister himself because they are too big, too urgent or too secret to go through a Cabinet Committee. One example is the Chancellor's outline of his budget, which will normally be the only item on the agenda.

Another example was the decision to devalue the pound in November 1967. This naturally did not appear on the agenda: in order to preserve secrecy a normal agenda had been circulated which was scrapped when the Cabinet met.

Major issues of policy that concern all or practically all departments go direct to the Cabinet. It would be dilatory and repetitious to take such a matter through a committee first: for all Ministers would have to be invited and the committee would therefore become in fact a Cabinet; and then the matter would have to go before the Cabinet again.

An example was the large Government programme of economies in January 1968. Although such a matter would not be sent to a committee, it would be very thoroughly prepared. The Chancellor of the Exchequer would circulate a paper giving his target of savings and indicating how it could be reached by particular departmental cuts. Each departmental Minister would have talks with the Chancellor, who might possibly moderate his first proposals.

When the whole programme comes before the Cabinet, each proposal for a departmental economy would be discussed in turn and separately decided. The Cabinet is always conscious in regard to such matters that each saving forms part of a packet which must in the end be decided upon as a whole. Tacitly or explicitly Ministers who accept or bow to cuts in their Estimates reserve the right to reopen the issue if savings proposed by the Chancellor in other fields are reduced by the Cabinet.

Some matters, even though they first go through a committee in order to ensure that all departmentally interested Ministers have had their say, always by their nature go before the Cabinet.

Certain of these come up at regular seasonal intervals: for instance the Defence White Paper (which goes through the Overseas Policy and Defence Committee); and the Farm Price Review (which goes through the Agricultural Policy Committee and on which it is assumed there will be disagreement between the Treasury and the Agricultural Ministers).

Other matters that undergo prolonged discussion in standing or ad hoc committees are of such importance that it is all along taken for granted that they will in due course be put on the Cabinet agenda. Examples of these are: the introduction of a scheme of income-related social insurance, which was worked out over two or three years in a committee; House of Lords reform; the Stansted airport.

Some issues are, so to speak, blown on to the Cabinet by their suddenness and importance: such, for instance, as the imminence of war between Arab states and Israel in June 1967; the decision to proclaim a Bank Holiday in March 1968; the Russian invasion of Czechoslovakia in August 1968. Often matters such as these have to be discussed without the aid of prepared papers: even a formal agenda may not have been circulated.

(3) Ministers' Initiatives

Far the greater number of items get on to the Cabinet agenda as the result of policies initiated by Ministers in their departments.

A Minister may know from the beginning that a policy he proposes is of such a nature that it is certain to go to a Cabinet Committee and very possibly to the Cabinet; if for instance it involves a White Paper.

But a Minister will perhaps not consider until his proposals are fairly fully elaborated how he will bring them before his colleagues.

When he comes to announce them publicly it may well not be apparent by what process within the Cabinet machine they came to fruition.

A Minister may consider that the matter is one that falls within his own competence to decide. He may be satisfied if other departments concerned are sounded out at official level. He may have a word with a few other Ministers, the Law Officers, or the Prime Minister. Any of these may suggest that the matter should go to the appropriate Cabinet Committee: the Minister may himself have decided on his own to proceed in this way.

These may not be easy matters for a Minister. If he takes too many questions to Cabinet Committees or straight to the Cabinet, he will be open to the criticism that he is indecisive and wishes overmuch to shelter behind his colleagues. He may encounter still stronger resentment if he has failed to bring before his colleagues questions which turn out to be politically embarrassing.

The first step towards bringing a matter before the Cabinet is for a Minister to take his proposals to the appropriate committee. Whether or not a particular issue will in due course make its way on to the Cabinet agenda is often at this stage unpredictable.

As I have pointed out above (Chapter 3, p. 43), Cabinet Committees are parallel and equal to the Cabinet itself. On matters within their terms of reference, committees can come to a decision that has the same authority as a Conclusion of the Cabinet: it will be accepted and acted upon as if it were a Cabinet decision.

An indefinite borderland therefore lies between the Cabinet and its committees. So far as the effectiveness of a decision goes, it matters not on which side of the line it falls.

If a Minister decides to bring a matter to a Cabinet Committee, a paper is prepared in his department for circulation to the members of the committee: the department concerts with the Secretary of the committee the day and hour when it shall come before the relevant committee.

The Minister will introduce and speak to his paper. Other Ministers may have circulated counter-papers or, if they are against the proposed policy, may prefer to criticize it from a brief.

How Things get to the Cabinet

The chairman must preside impartially, but may enter as strongly as he wishes into the merits of a matter. After, in his view, sufficient argument has occurred and the committee is ready, he sums up.

It is the chairman's duty to try and settle things in committee and as far as possible save the time of the Cabinet. There may be such a clear consensus for or against the Minister's proposals that he can state this in his conclusions. If disagreement persists the chairman may suggest that the Minister should take his paper back and reconsider it in the light of the discussion; or perhaps, if there are two or three Ministers who are mainly in conflict, that they should talk things over and try and reconcile their differences: in such cases the matter would come back later to the committee. The chairman may state in his conclusion that the question is so important or the differences are so deep that it must clearly go to the Cabinet.

It may be that the Chairman's conclusion, whether for or against a Minister's proposals, may be contested by one or more members of the committee. Since Mr Harold Wilson's ruling in 1967 (see Chapter 3, p. 46), no Minister can without the chairman's consent take a matter from committee to Cabinet. The chairman may say that he will have a word with the Prime Minister. The aggrieved Minister can himself appeal to the Prime Minister, who in such cases of dispute alone determines whether the issue should go to the Cabinet.

When I was chairman of the Home Affairs Committee and the Social Services Committee, I was generally able to get matters settled in the committees. If there was disagreement, I tended in summing up to weight the balance in favour of Cabinet Ministers as against non-Cabinet or junior Ministers. Should the question go to the Cabinet, it would be the Cabinet Ministers on the committee who would be best informed and most involved.

It can happen that a Cabinet Committee has a second go at a paper even if it is not taken back to be rewritten. When I was in the chair of the Home Affairs Committee a paper put in by a Cabinet Minister was expounded, in his absence, by a junior Minister. The committee by a clear consensus rejected the proposals. Thereupon the Cabinet Minister strongly represented to me as chairman that he would like the paper reconsidered. In order to try and avoid the Prime Minister and perhaps the Cabinet being troubled, I agreed. The Minister, armed with knowledge of the points that had been put against his paper, argued so strongly and persuasively that the committee endorsed the paper.

The chairman can, at his discretion, accept a request by a member of the committee to raise by correspondence with the other members some minor change in a paper that has already been accepted by the committee. If, as is almost always the case, no member objects, the committee is deemed to have amended the previous Conclusion and all interested departments are informed.

By this flexible process it is determined on which side of the indefinite frontier between committee and Cabinet an issue may lie.

Certain issues can reach the Cabinet by a quite different route and without previous passage through a committee.

These are matters of such importance that they must evidently come before the Cabinet and be settled there, but which need very careful and detailed preparation.

It was to deal with matters of this kind that the practice arose of servicing the Cabinet itself by committees of officials.

In 1951 Sir Stafford Cripps submitted to the Cabinet an official paper a couple of inches thick that contained immensely detailed briefs for our representatives at the Japanese peace conference. Cripps admitted that he had had no time to read it closely: he realized that other members of the Cabinet could not do so: and asked us to take the paper on trust.

In Mr Harold Wilson's Cabinets the practice of using committees of officials grew in frequency and importance; particularly in connection with the series of Cabinet debates in May 1967 on the question of applying for membership of the Common Market.

So complex and interlocked were the issues involved that these debates were conducted on the basis of papers, nearly all of which were prepared by a committee of officials made up of Permanent Heads of the relevant departments. Ministers were able, if they wished – as a few did—to influence these official papers by giving instructions to their own departmental officials.

At the six or seven Cabinet meetings which discussed the Common Market issue, it was the sole item on the agenda: though several papers on different aspects of the problem might be taken at one meeting.

CHAPTER 8

THE DECISION TO WITHDRAW FROM EAST OF SUEZ

(1) The First Line-up

In this chapter I single out the process by which the Cabinet took one particular decision, which involved the most momentous shift in our foreign policy for a century and a half—namely the decision to withdraw from East of Suez.

In the eye of history it may well appear that this revolution in Britain's defence posture was but the recognition of forces that had been long at work. In both world wars Britain had concentrated her major effort on the continent of Europe. During and after the second war her relative power had been transformed by the rise of two super powers and by the tide of nationalism which challenged all alien rule, whether Western or communist.

Yet not until January 1968 was the Cabinet decision to abandon bases East of Suez announced to Parliament.

The decision was taken by a Labour Cabinet after thirteen years of Conservative rule, during which time the Government never seems to have examined the question: a British role East of Suez was taken for granted.

The radical change of policy was not, however, an automatic or doctrinal consequence of a change of Administration. The Cabinet came to its conclusion with reluctance after the Labour Government had been over three years in office.

Initially the mind of the Labour Cabinet was clearly for maintaining the existing British presence East of Suez.

In the light of later developments one can perhaps retrospectively identify two embryonic groups in the Cabinet (whose views by no means coincided) who were inclined to favour at least a scrutiny of the Far East policy. The 'economizers' were conscious of the burden that our commitments East of Suez placed upon the budget and the balance of payments. Those, still in a minority, who supported British entry into the Common Market tended to be temperamentally against policies that distracted our attention from Europe and looked with little favour upon too much concern with the views of other Common-wealth countries. Some scarcely perceptible influence was exerted on the Cabinet by the small vocal section in the Parliamentary Labour Party who were against all defence expenditure and who concentrated their first fire upon the more vulnerable commitments East of Suez.

Such views as these were neither concrete nor coherent enough to crystallize into a challenge against the conclusions of the 'strategists' – the Ministers primarily concerned with overseas and defence policy. Broadly and with varying degrees of conscious articulation, these adhered to what may be called an Indian Ocean strategy.

This ocean gives access to India, Australia, New Zealand and the East African members of the Commonwealth. Domination of the Indian Ocean involved control of its two gateways – Singapore and the Persian Gulf – and of Aden which commanded the route to them. Further arguments for holding the Persian Gulf were that it was the source of a great deal of our oil: and that, if we withdrew, a vacuum would be created which might tempt Irak, Persia, Saudi Arabia, Egypt and perhaps Russia – with resultant chaos.

There was an uneasy feeling that this strategy rested upon bases that might prove untenable: it was generally taken for granted in the Cabinet that no overseas base could be usefully held against the con-tinuing and active opposition of the local population.

These incipient doubts and the different tendencies of thought in the Cabinet did not come to open expression: indeed they can only with hindsight be detected because they later became lustier and more vocal.

At the time all questions and inquietudes were stilled by Indonesia's aggressive confrontation with Malaysia. This had started in August 1964 and the new Labour Cabinet continued without question the military succour of Malaysia. This committed the Cabinet to an East of Suez policy: the considerable forces in Malaysia could not be sustained without holding Aden, the Persian Gulf and Singapore.

Other factors helped to suppress open questioning of the East of Suez policy in the Cabinet.

Comfort was taken from the thought that British occupation of the overseas bases brought considerable economic benefit to the inhabitants and that our withdrawal would only expose them to the danger of being taken over by less benevolent rulers. Surely they could be brought to see where their true interests lay.

Memories were still fresh of the way in which we had come to Kuwait's aid at her request in 1961: and, in January 1964, had promptly answered the call for military help to suppress army mutinies in Kenya, Uganda and Tanganyika. None of these actions would have been possible but for our presence East of Suez.

Remembrance of these things—flattering to a country that was making its final withdrawals in the face of nationalist movements—was a vivid and doubt-quietening factor in the minds of Ministers.

That the Cabinet was influenced by the pressure exerted by the United States upon Britain to stay in the Far East is a myth.

Mr Dean Rusk, the Secretary of State, had as a Rhodes Scholar at Oxford written a thesis on the Commonwealth. Ever after, he had a slightly distorted picture of the Commonwealth as a group of nations that were in some sense led or represented by Britain: somehow Britain's presence East of Suez would imply the presence of other members of the Commonwealth.

Even with a different Secretary of State, America's main motive would have remained—namely a desire not to be left as a lonely gendarme in the Far East. Britain's bases strategically fitted into and underpinned the deployment of United States forces.

Mr Dean Rusk on a number of occasions told me and other British Ministers who visited him that in America's eyes a British soldier East of Suez was more valuable than one in Germany. When, however, the argument was pushed to its conclusion, it appeared that America was just as keen not to be left in isolation in Europe.

Sometimes, when the issue of our presence East of Suez finally arose in the Cabinet, the point was put that this presence gave us influence over America. But American pressure was not a factor in the Cabinet's resolve to continue to hold our bases. It was occasionally prayed in aid only because Britain had for her own reasons settled on this policy.

Far heavier American pressure was exerted to persuade us to make even a token military contribution to the war in Vietnam: President Johnson forcibly explained that it was not the number of troops that he was concerned about, but the number of 'flags' represented by units, however small, from different nations. He wanted a show of support which would connote a moral attitude. This persistent pressure was resolutely resisted.

More influential was Commonwealth pressure from Australia, New Zealand, Malaysia and Singapore – both in itself and because it found a significant echo in political opinion in Britain. This was a factor that played some part in complicating the decision to abandon our bases East of Suez.

It is possible to detect, even at this early stage, some vague and incipient doubts about the long-term implications of the East of Suez policy: but these were long in crystallizing and expressing themselves.

The change of Government in 1964 made no perceptible impact upon policy. The Cabinet in its first Defence White Paper in February 1965 stated:

> Britain must, to meet her obligations to Commonwealth and allied countries, maintain a capacity for providing military assistance in many parts of the world.

These words closely echoed those of the last Conservative Defence White Paper twelve months earlier. The chief differences were that the Labour Cabinet hoped to carry out the policy more cheaply: and that 'we recognize that [the overseas bases] can be maintained only in agreement with the local governments and peoples.'

(2) The Shift of Opinion

From this starting point – some twenty years after the end of the second world war—the balance of opinion in the Cabinet began gradually to shift.

Opinion in favour of entry into the Common Market gathered strength: economic crises and runs on the pound reinforced the arguments of the 'economizers'. These two factors combined to raise more vigorously questions about the validity of the East of Suez policy. How could we ever get out of our balance of payments problem whilst we spent so much across the exchanges on defence? Why should Britain pursue policies so different from those of other equivalent European powers—and so much more costly? Why should we not, like other European countries, obtain oil from the Persian Gulf by paying for it instead of maintaining forces there?

Simultaneously doubts began to grow about the effectiveness of our presence East of Suez in securing and protecting our interests.

These points were not specifically raised or argued in the Cabinet. In so far as they came up it was in relation to different aspects of policy: the connection between decisions or views in one field and those in another did not become apparent.

The prevailing view remained in favour of maintaining the East of Suez policy: but the beginning of a shift of attitude showed itself in a change in the arguments used to justify such a policy.

Greater emphasis was laid upon the need for further economies in defence: alternatives to the maintenance of expensive and perhaps untenable mainland bases began to be worked out. Along these lines a kind of compromise was established between the various views in the Cabinet and in the Overseas Policy and Defence Committee: existing policy would be continued on a basis that was less costly and therefore more tolerable and acceptable.

The compromise was adumbrated in the Defence White Paper of February 1966. It was announced that Aden should become independent by the end of 1968 and all British forces withdrawn thence. This and other savings, it was claimed, would cut by sixteen per cent the expenditure originally contemplated by the Conservative Government for this year. The most significant feature of the White Paper was that it threw out the idea for the first time of a base in Australia as an alternative to existing bases. In the previous November, as part of this alternative strategic notion, the British Indian Ocean Territory was proclaimed as a new British colony. Talks were proceeding with the Americans about the joint development in this oceanic colony of a staging post that would enable us to reach Australia without reliance on mainland bases.

Within a few months – in July 1966 – a serious economic crisis occurred that induced the Cabinet to propose a number of savings, including the decision to build no more aircraft carriers. The imminence of this decision had led to the resignation in February 1966 of Mr Mayhew, the Minister of Defence (Royal Navy), and an admiral on the ground that we would no longer have the tools to carry out our East of Suez policy. A month later, in August, the Indonesian confrontation with Malaysia came to a final end after petering out over the previous two or three months.

These were turning points. None the less the Cabinet remained as reluctant as ever to abandon its East of Suez policy.

In February 1967 the Defence White Paper declared:

> The continued presence of British forces can help to create an environment, in which local governments are able to establish the political and economic basis for peace and stability. There can be no certainty ... that these forces will not be required to help friendly governments ... as they have done in recent years.

The memory of Kuwait and the East African mutinies was still a factor in the Cabinet's policy.

The independence of Aden was advanced by a year to November 1967. Although this would knock out the route to the Persian Gulf, an increase in the British forces there was announced.

The White Paper spoke with greater force and clarity of a base in Australia and of:

> the benefits we would get from a new staging airfield in the British Indian Ocean Territory ... [which] would offer us greater

flexibility in our future defence planning, particularly in relation to the Far East.

In April 1967 an agreement with America for the joint development of a staging post was published.

The high point in the justification of the Cabinet's East of Suez policy came in March 1967. In the House of Commons sixty-three Labour M.P.s voted against the Defence White Paper. Mr Harold Wilson at once addressed a meeting of the Parliamentary Labour Party. 'He turned savagely on the sixty-three rebels' (*The Times*, March 3rd, 1967); and made a powerful and scathing speech in justification of the East of Suez policy along the lines of the White Paper.

At this very moment forces and factors began to gather and accumulate which were to lead in a matter of months to a complete reversal of policy.

Between January and March 1967 Mr Harold Wilson was making his tour of European capitals to explore the way into the Common Market. During this time and for some weeks after, the Cabinet was heavily engaged in discussing the question of applying for membership.

A clear shift of opinion in favour of application was apparent. Some Ministers were won over by argument and by the views of the Prime Minister and Foreign Secretary. Some came round because of the continuing weakening of the pound and the need to save overseas expenditure by a radical change in defence policy.

On May 2nd, 1967 the Cabinet's decision to apply for membership of the European Economic Community was announced to Parliament and shortly thereafter endorsed by both Houses.

The movement of opinion in the Cabinet in favour of entry into the Common Market marked an equivalent trend away from support of the East of Suez policy: it temperamentally implied a recognition that Britain was a European and not a world power.

But, as was clear from Mr Harold Wilson's tough talk to the Parliamentary Labour Party—at the very time when he was completing his tour of continental capitals—the two things were not directly or intellectually related. Each policy was being separately considered in the Cabinet.

In June 1967 occurred the six-day Arab-Israeli war. Our inability to prevent it (which came out starkly in sharp and angry Cabinet debates); to affect its course; or to do anything about the subsequent Arab reprisals against our trade and our supplies of oil – all this greatly strengthened the already growing conviction in the Cabinet that our presence East of Suez was both vain and costly.

The first open indication of a change of policy came in the supplementary Defence White Paper of July 1967:

> We have taken into account major developments in the last twelve months: political – the evolution of government policy towards Europe … and economic – a more pressing need to reduce overseas expenditure.

On these grounds the Cabinet was 'planning' the withdrawal of our troops from outside Europe. For the first time the White Paper spoke of a 'military capacity' instead of a presence in the Far East.

The general line was clear: but these were still future perspectives. No specific or dated decision seemed to be called for: and none was announced.

(3) The Decision

Devaluation in November 1967 was the traumatic shock.

Economic emergency compelled the Cabinet to face a radical alteration of defence policy: it made articulate a decision that had, as it were, subconsciously been reached; but which the Cabinet as a whole and the Prime Minister had flinched from recognizing.

Devaluation automatically added fifty million pounds a year to defence costs. Immediate cuts had therefore to be made. As part of the savings announced at the same time as devaluation was the abandonment of the staging post in the British Indian Ocean Territory – only two years after the proclamation of the new British colony and seven months after the publication of the agreement with America for a joint staging post. Thereby was buried the still-born notion of an Australian base. These abortive plans were but empty memorials to the attempts of a reluctant Cabinet to find alternative means to carry out an East of Suez strategy.

The Cabinet at once set about working out a package of economies. Defence expenditure had to be heavily cut: partly to balance severe savings in the social services; partly to enable the Cabinet to reach its total target for reductions in public spending.

Thus it came about that in January 1968 the Prime Minister announced to Parliament, as part and parcel of a whole series of Government economies, the historic decision of the Cabinet to abandon Britain's East of Suez policy.

A month later, the Defence White Paper of February 1968 spelled out the implications of the decision. Withdrawal from East of Suez was now dated: it would be completed by the end of 1971.

> Britain's defence effort will in future be concentrated mainly in Europe and the North Atlantic.

A mere gesture was made towards the needs of Commonwealth countries. A *general capability* for deployment overseas now replaced the already attenuated *military capability*: and this would now operate only if *in our judgment circumstances demand.*

The first complete statement of the new strategy occurred in the Defence White Paper of February 1969. In a significant phrase it spoke of a concentration of our military effort *West of Suez*. No capability of any kind was claimed for the deployment of forces overseas: all that was left was:

> good progress in planning new arrangements to help preserve stability ... after we have withdrawn from our mainland bases East of Suez.

(4) The Decision in Perspective

Such were the steps leading to the great decision and to the full acceptance of its implications.

Faltering enough they seem. The decision appears so reluctant as to have been unintended until almost the last moment. The Cabinet looks as if it were pushed and coerced by unforeseen events into an unwelcome conclusion. Factors and policies that were clearly linked were not correlated.

Was this apparent lack of clarity and decision due to, or intensified by, the Cabinet Committee system? The purpose of this system is to allow many decisions to be simultaneously processed and reached. To prevent friction and waste of time and effort, each committee must concentrate on the questions and problems that fall within its terms of reference. But the committee system has built-in safeguards against a failure to co-ordinate policy: the membership of committees is overlapping; Cabinet Ministers will be on two or three major committees — sometimes ones with which they have no departmental interest. Moreover, the Conclusions of Cabinet Committees are circulated to Cabinet Ministers and other Ministers concerned: in particular the Prime Minister, aided by the Cabinet Secretary, keeps a watch over them.

In fact, in the case we are considering, all the great issues having a hearing on the decision to withdraw from East of Suez were considered and settled in the Cabinet itself. Defence White Papers were elaborated and drafted in the Overseas Policy and Defence Committee: but, like all White Papers, they were gone over in detail, sometimes altered, and approved by the Cabinet. Proposals for savings in defence expenditure were similarly handled. In any case the terms of reference of this committee embraced overseas policy as well as defence.

All aspects of entry into the Common Market were discussed at length and in detail in a series of Cabinet meetings. So were the major economies made at various times of financial crisis.

Thus if reasons are sought for the apparently inconsequent and dilatory progress towards the great decision, they must be found in the Cabinet. Does this disclose a defect in the nature of Cabinet government?

I think not. If this conclusion appears to emerge from our discussion, it is because we have been asking a wrong question about the Cabinet.

It is useful and illuminating to try and trace out the steps by which an important decision was reached by the Cabinet. But this throws more light on the decision than on the actual working of the Cabinet.

The search for the course and causes of any specific decision must

131

distort reality. It presupposes the isolation of an issue from its background: an isolation of which no Cabinet or any other decision-making apparatus is capable.

In real life a Cabinet is not considering one issue, however great. It must face, discuss and resolve a great mass of problems simultaneously. The connection between them may vary: but all questions before the Cabinet are in some degree interacting. They are running side by side. Each of them may widen or lessen or shift the divisions in the Cabinet and influence the relationship between its members: and thus alter the balance within the Cabinet when another decision falls to be made. Each decision may have an impact upon party, Parliament and public that may well affect expected reactions to later decisions.

All these and other factors are among the considerations — some of them intangible and unspoken — in the minds of members of the Cabinet as they discuss and reconsider such an issue as policy East of Suez. Ministers are very conscious of the interconnection between issues: one reason why they may not clearly detect the interconnection between various factors affecting an isolated issue is that they connect them all together in a living and continuing nexus.

It would be easier and simpler for students of the Cabinet system if the Cabinet were a detached body of men united in aloof wisdom. It is not and cannot be any such thing: it is not, cannot be, and should not be, capable of sitting back and looking at things in prospect as they can be looked back to after they have moved into the past.

A Cabinet must contain conflicting views and shifting trends of opinion. These, in turn, must be influenced by the advice of military and other experts; they must reflect and interact with views in the party, in the House and in the press.

A Cabinet that sat back considering one issue whilst neglecting other pressing matters would be failing in its prime duty as the seat of political authority. A Cabinet detached from its political context — if such a thing were possible under any system of government — would in a parliamentary democracy be a monstrosity.

However complex and perhaps inextricable are the pressures and

problems, rivalries and reactions that operate in and upon the Cabinet —
it must none the less, if it is to govern well, be capable of taking great
decisions in a coherent way and with appropriate despatch.

Did the Cabinet fulfil its duty in this way in regard to the decision to
abandon our East of Suez strategy: or did it fail?

The critical test and question is this — was the decision improperly,
incompetently and unduly delayed?

If we consider on a broader and more concentrated time-scale the
same question that I have here attempted to analyse — it emerges that
*the Cabinet came to the decision to withdraw from East of Suez at the
earliest moment when such a policy became practical.*

Indonesian confrontation with Malaysia did not end till June 1966
and was not formally concluded until August. During that time Aden
and the Persian Gulf had to be held to give access to Singapore and
Malaysia. Within little over a year after the end of confrontation, the
complex and dangerous process of disengagement from Aden was
carried through. The last British troops left at the end of November 1967.

Within less than two months of that the abandonment of the East of
Suez policy was announced.

In retrospect there seems little logic in the proclamation in
November 1965 of the British Indian Ocean Territory as a new colony
and the abandonment two years later of the staging post which was its
sole purpose: or in the decision in February 1967 to increase forces in
the Persian Gulf after the decision to leave Aden. Mr Harold Wilson's
sharp defence of the East of Suez policy in March 1967 seems not to fit
into a consequent pattern of decision.

Yet all these actions may have contributed to the extraordinary
conclusion to this story.

An epoch-making and revolutionary decision, taken at the earliest
possible time, was widely accepted both at home and in the Commonwealth countries principally and critically concerned.

Such a conclusion and neither tidiness of decision nor detached fore-
sight are the proof that in this momentous matter the Cabinet system
worked pretty well in the political environment of which it is an
integral part.

CHAPTER 9

CABINET DEBATES

(1) Cabinet Meeting, 1950

I attended my first Cabinet in 1950 in the Prime Minister's room in the House of Commons. We were meeting there because we had a majority of only six — then an unprecedentedly small one. An Opposition amendment to the Queen's Speech was being moved and we had to be on hand to vote.

ATTLEE. We may be defeated tonight. If so, in my view we should resign.

A silence followed. As the most junior member I hesitated to speak in case someone else wanted to. After a time, I said: 'Prime Minister, I am not sure. I am inclined to think that all serious votes in the House should carry their consequences. If defeated, we should think in terms of another immediate general election.'

HERBERT MORRISON. Prime Minister, in view of what the Commonwealth Secretary has said, I think we should wait until the Foreign Secretary is here. He has been slightly delayed.

Ernest Bevin arrived soon after. It appeared that he and Herbert Morrison had had a word together on the matter.

ATTLEE. Foreign Secretary, we have put off till your arrival consideration of what we should do if we are defeated tonight.

Ernest Bevin then strongly and robustly stated the view that I had raised. After a brief discussion this was accepted as the policy of the Cabinet.

134

(2) Bevan's Resignation

Extract from my diary—April 9th, 1951.

Today we had a major Government crisis about the budget. We had a meeting in the morning at No. 10. Herbert Morrison presided. At the end it was suggested that we should meet again that evening as the Prime Minister, who was in hospital, should be consulted.

We met at six thirty p.m. in the Prime Minister's room in the House of Commons. The Prime Minister had sent a message that the Cabinet must stand firm. Bevan now said that he disliked the whole defence programme and that when a man felt he had more power outside the Cabinet than in, he should resign. He was a prisoner.

Wilson for the first time said he would resign too. Bevan: 'He has been very loyal and I release him.'

We took a formal vote, each person in order round the table saying Yes or No—yes meaning that we favoured Gaitskell's budget proposals. All voted yes except Bevan and Wilson; and Tomlinson, who still wanted delay, for which he had spoken all along.

(3) Two Meetings of Ministers, 1949

(a) Extract from diary January 7th, 1949 (when I was Parliamentary Under Secretary for Commonwealth Relations).

A most important meeting of the Commonwealth Affairs Committee of the Cabinet at No. 10 at eleven fifteen this morning. Prime Minister, Cripps, Bevin, Noel-Baker, Jowitt, Shawcross, Addison and Creech-Jones. All the three papers before them had been written by me: an unsigned report of a talk between P.M., Cripps and Krishna Menon [the Indian High Commissioner]; a signed note on the Commonwealth Citizenship idea originally put forward by Krishna; a memorandum on my idea of a new approach to the problem of India's membership of the Commonwealth—'The Link with India'.

The discussion started with Bevin saying in effect that the Commonwealth ought to be dissolved. His officials had been at him: they are sore at Indian and Australian resentment over our attitude towards the Dutch aggression in Indonesia and over Evatt's [Australian Minister of

External Affairs] escapades. At the bottom of their hearts they think they could run foreign policy better than we can run Commonwealth relations: they want ambassadors under direct instructions. But others attacked him and Noel-Baker gave a child's guide lecture on the Commonwealth. Later Bevin came round and began to help.

My paper on India was in effect the main subject of discussion. The Prime Minister called on me to speak towards the end and I gave my views strongly. The Crown-link with India is out. Let's fit in India as a republic, based on the reality of a common act of will. Then let's add embellishments, which could become valuable – though they are dangerous if we try to *constitute* the link out of them.

Shawcross attacked this on the ground that unless we had the common crown or common nationality it would not stand up under international law. Cripps and the Prime Minister in effect said that law must be made for people and international law must adjust itself.

It was decided that officials should work these ideas out. I must try and get my hands on this.

(b) Extract from diary, February 9th, 1949.

Yesterday and again today two meetings of Ministers to discuss question of India's membership of the Commonwealth – Prime Minister, Jowitt, Noel-Baker, Addison, Creech-Jones and Shawcross. Norman Brook [Secretary of the Cabinet] played a considerable part: he and I agree. Liesching [Permanent Head of Commonwealth Office] also attended.

We had a paper before us which largely embodied my ideas. Its whole basis was to fit India into the Commonwealth openly as a republic. I was the first to put this forward as an official idea. Its particular proposal is to base membership on simple declarations (i) by India, saying it wanted to stay in the Commonwealth, (ii) by all the other countries saying they agreed. This was not in the original draft, but was put in after a paper I had written. Another idea that I put forward only verbally was adopted during the discussion, namely that we should send emissaries to Commonwealth countries.

At the first meeting the Prime Minister asked me to speak. I said I had no doubt India should be fitted in: we must give time a chance. There had been a rapid development of feeling towards Britain: recently even the Congress Party had voted for association. I thought it would strengthen not weaken the Crown to keep it only where it had reality. I favoured the two simultaneous declarations, rather than an attempt to redefine the Commonwealth. We needed two things: to limit the Commonwealth to those who had been in it; and to base membership on a declared act of will.

Bevin argued the Foreign Office line – that it was not worth keeping India in the Commonwealth: it was not going to be morally committed to us, but we to it. To keep India in would lead to the breakdown of the old Commonwealth. In the course of the discussion, Bevin warmed up and made some positive suggestions.

Jowitt wobbled. Addison kept clearly in mind the need to keep India in. Shawcross overpressed the legal arguments but admitted that they must be subordinated to political ones. He had a clear preference for a 'compact Commonwealth' bound by the legal reality of allegiance to the Crown.

The Prime Minister was most impressive. He fully realizes the difficulties of the King, the Opposition and other Commonwealth countries. He does not rush. But he moves the argument steadily forward, allowing it to repeat itself a good deal – perhaps too much. He wants India in; he realizes the value of time: but also the need to press forward now.

The value even of stupid and repetitive discussion is clear. It allows a gradual shaping of policy.

At the end it was decided to get a working party of officials to look into the effects of India leaving the Commonwealth, with or without a treaty – and keeping her in: in terms of most-favoured nation treatment, citizenship and the like. The basic paper is to be prepared in terms suitable to be sent to the other Commonwealth countries. On my suggestion, officials are also to work out a timetable. I think we will send emissaries round in about a month and have a Prime Ministers' meeting by April.

(4) Imaginary Cabinet Meeting (Foreign Affairs)

PRIME MINISTER. I have called this meeting at very short notice. You all know what it's about—the seizure of our uranium deposits and works by the Government of Lorentia. I'm afraid there's been no time to prepare papers—things have just been happening too fast. I'll ask the Foreign Secretary to put the Cabinet in the picture.

FOREIGN SECRETARY. Prime Minister, we are faced with a grave and difficult situation. I have thought a great deal and very anxiously about the advice I should give my colleagues. But before coming to that—let me bring the Cabinet up to date about the latest situation. I was up to a very late hour last night reading the telegrams as they came in: I was woken up once by the Office in the middle of the night: I saw the latest telegrams this morning. So, Prime Minister, if my account isn't in the best logical order, I hope my colleagues will forgive me.

The latest situation is that the strike in Ariadne, where our works are, is still going on. I now have firm information, from sources I don't want to mention, that this strike was fomented and organized by the new Government of Lorentia—

MINISTER OF LIBRARIES. When did the strike start?

FOREIGN SECRETARY. About a week ago. Two days ago the Government started riots among the strikers. Yesterday Government officials came to the offices of British Uranium and told the managing director that the company had been sequestered by the Government of Lorentia and that he must leave the office at once. He protested, but left when the officials threatened to bring in soldiers to arrest him. He went to our Consul who has been in constant touch with us ever since. He has kept his head and is doing a good job. We have found out through him that there are about eighty British subjects in the uranium field, including about fifteen women and the same number of children. In the town of Ariadne there are several hundred more. I have told the Consul to advise the women and children to make at once for Ariadne. The men, according to the Consul, don't want to leave and I haven't yet told him to give them any advice, pending this meeting of the Cabinet.

MINISTER OF INVESTMENT. I'm sorry to interrupt, Prime Minister, but could the Foreign Secretary tell us if our people are safe in Ariadne itself?

FOREIGN SECRETARY: Yes, I should have mentioned that. I'm obliged. The answer is that they appear so far to be in no immediate danger. All British staff except the managing director are still in the works: but owing to the strike there's nothing they can do except do their best to keep safety precautions going. Quite a large number live together in the compound and these could hold out for a time if attacked. Others live scattered about the town. Nothing has happened to them yet. Is that what you wanted to know, Minister of Investment?

Besides the very great British interests directly involved, there are wider aspects of this crisis, Prime Minister, that cause me very great concern. Lorentia's neighbour, Alcidan, has always laid claim to the area to the west of Ariadne. The present instability of the Government of Lorentia may tempt Alcidan to move into this area. Alcidan has recently been scared of an attack by Lorentia upon the small islands which command the straits of Ariadne. This would amount to a blockade of Alcidan. Our latest information is that, just because of its present nationalist fervour, Lorentia may be about to launch such a military operation. Alcidan may well strike first to forestall such an operation. The danger of hostilities is great. Both sides have made warlike noises and moved troops forward. That's the situation. It's a threatening one and if hostilities broke out, our interests would be further hit. Our trade with both these countries and with the whole area is very considerable.

My greatest fear is that the war would spread. Russia is pouring in arms. The war might reach a stage at which we couldn't keep out.

What should we do? We can't dodge a decision one way or the other. If we do nothing, that too is a decision: and it could lead to a spread of the war with the possible consequences I have described. If we act, we will protect British interests and keep the peace.

I've given long and anxious thought to this, Prime Minister, and I spoke to you about it this morning. I have come to the conclusion that we ought to send naval units to the Ariadne estuary. The Defence Secretary will be able to tell us about the logistics. I want as many marines on board as possible. We would then be able to rescue British subjects at need: and we would be in a position to seize back our works. But most important of all, we would have ships between Lorentia and the islands. The only thing that can, in my judgment, prevent war is to give Alcidan a visible British guarantee against attack. The presence of British ships would be such a guarantee.

At the same time we should take steps at the U.N. to prevent an outbreak of hostilities between Alcidan and Lorentia. I would like my colleagues' authority to try and get a resolution through the Security Council and the General Assembly calling on both countries to keep the peace and sending an observer team to the area. If hostilities break out, we should get a resolution calling for a cease-fire. I should tell the Cabinet that I have alerted our Ambassadors and High Commissioners in countries represented in the United Nations to go into action and urge the need for speedy and effective action in New York.

I am sorry to spring these vigorous proposals upon the Cabinet without preparation. I had to do so because we must quickly decide one way or the other. There are risks in my policy. I know that. You needn't tell me. But there are risks whatever we do. I beg any of my colleagues who may be reluctant to accept my suggestions to think what might happen if we do nothing. The habit of seizing British property might spread: British lives may be lost. If fighting starts between Alcidan and Lorentia, the war may spread in a very dangerous way that might draw us in. We would suffer heavy economic loss—much worse than the seizure of our works in Ariadne. I for one am not prepared to run *those* risks.

PRIME MINISTER. Secretary of State for Defence, could you tell us about the military aspect of the Foreign Secretary's proposals?

DEFENCE SECRETARY. Yes, Prime Minister. I consulted the Chiefs of Staff immediately after our talk with the Foreign Secretary this morning. We have sufficient naval forces in or near the area. We could get some ships there in twenty-four hours. We have not enough marines within reach: but we could embark a couple of infantry battalions at Port Pontino. That is why it would take us three days to get effective forces to Ariadne. That's what you might call the pure logistics—but I'm afraid there's more in it than that. We couldn't send large ships close inshore: they would be sitting ducks in these narrow waters to shore batteries, torpedoes and aircraft. We could send in small ships: but what would happen if they were fired on? They could probably look after themselves: but we couldn't reinforce them. All they could do would be to return fire and withdraw. A shipborne military operation in well-guarded narrow waters is a nonsense. I can see the logic of the Foreign Secretary's policy but there's no way of giving naval teeth to it.

FOREIGN SECRETARY. But, Secretary of State for Defence, why have you so suddenly changed your mind? I didn't think *you* were a wobbler. Only this morning you agreed with me and the Prime Minister—if anything you rather pushed me along.

DEFENCE SECRETARY. Prime Minister, I would like to support the Foreign Secretary. I want the same things as he does. But after our meeting I consulted my expert advisers and have come to the conclusion that what seemed politically attractive this morning is in fact militarily unattainable. That's all there is to it.

PRIME MINISTER. Chancellor of the Exchequer, what about the financial and economic aspects?

CHANCELLOR OF THE EXCHEQUER. Well, Prime Minister, this has come rather suddenly upon me. I don't know as much as the Foreign Secretary and the Secretary of State for Defence seem to. But I am pretty clear in my own mind about the economic issues involved. It is true that the outbreak of fighting in the area, and even more its spread, would have an adverse effect on our balance of trade—though it would check imports as well as exports. Much the worst consequence would be the need to pay hard currency for the uranium that we wouldn't be getting from Lorentia. That is one thing we must look into right away—how far we can economize and where we can get alternative supplies from. On the other hand the course you and the Foreign Secretary propose, Prime Minister, would cost us a great deal of money and lead to higher taxation: but—

MINISTER OF INVESTMENT. I am sick and tired of the Chancellor's constant veto on everything we should do. I think we must stand by—

CHANCELLOR OF EXCHEQUER. Prime Minister, I had not finished. In a matter of this gravity each of us ought to be allowed to speak without interruption.

PRIME MINISTER. Go on, Chancellor. There will be time for everyone to speak.

CHANCELLOR OF THE EXCHEQUER. I was actually in the middle of a sentence. I was about to say that far graver than the budgetary cost would be the effect upon the pound. A disturbance of this kind in which we ourselves got involved could lead to a run on the pound. The outbreak of fighting would itself be bad enough: but if you add to this the upset of the international market, increased overseas expenditure and our need to raise taxes—well, the Foreign Secretary's proposals would involve us in an immediate economic crisis that would be worse than the effects of losing the uranium for a time.

PRIME MINISTER. Minister of Investment.

MINISTER OF INVESTMENT. I apologize to the Chancellor for interrupting him and getting a bit heated. But, Prime Minister, I feel very strongly on this issue. At the bottom of all the complications is a very simple principle. We can talk till we're blue in the face about dubious and doubtful economic consequences, but there are times when principles must come first. The fact is that Alcidan is a progressive, democratic state. It has many friends in this country, especially in the Churches. We ought to stand by it and make clear to Lorentia that we won't stand any nonsense. I am not sure about all the objectives of the Foreign Secretary's proposals: some of them seem problematical to me. But on the main point I'm with him. We ought to send the Navy in and prevent Lorentia from attacking Alcidan.

MINISTER FOR THE ISLES. ⎫
MINISTER WITH PORTFOLIO. ⎬ (together) – Prime Minister.

PRIME MINISTER: I want next to call the Minister of Nuclear Energy. What will be the effect of cutting off our supplies of uranium?

MINISTER OF NUCLEAR ENERGY. Prime Minister, I have begun to go into this question with my Office. I'm afraid we haven't got very far yet, as the whole thing is rather complex. We don't yet know how much uranium is en route: nor how much is already processed at Ariadne, which we might still get out. It is not uranium as such that matters in the short run. It's the plutonium that counts. It may be that we can economize here and eke out our supplies for quite a while. If the crisis goes on, we'll certainly have to pay dollars to keep up necessary supplies: but we may be able to scrape up a certain amount from other sources. That's all I have been able to find out in the short time at my disposal. I have set up a high-powered working party to go into the whole thing. I agree with the Chancellor that we must find out as quickly as possible where we stand. One thing that we ought to do at once is approach all Governments concerned to see that they don't buy uranium that belongs to us.

PRIME MINISTER. Minister with Portfolio.

MINISTER WITH PORTFOLIO. Prime Minister, I don't see how we can follow the simple line suggested by the Minister of Investment. We have been told that either of these countries may attack the other, we don't know which. They're on a par. A progressive state can be an aggressive state. The principle that matters is that aggression must be condemned whether or not it is committed by a state that we – or some of our people and some members of the

Cabinet—happen to like. We should not take sides. But I go further than that, Prime Minister. Fighting may indeed break out in this area, but why should we get involved? We have no duties or obligations here—all these countries are now independent. Why should we take enormous economic risks for something that doesn't concern us more than anyone else? We might well be involved in military risks, too. Once marines or troops are landed, we may have to send in more forces to extricate them. We may be in up to the neck before we are finished.

FOREIGN SECRETARY. Could I come in again, Prime Minister, just for a moment? The Minister with Portfolio thinks we should keep out. I frankly don't like his rather weak and neutralist line. But the real question is—can we keep out? If we intervene to protect British interests and lives and to prevent the spread of war we would certainly be involved in the way the Minister with Portfolio objects to. But say we follow his policy and do nothing, fold our hands, keep safe—and then fighting breaks out and spreads, we are also involved in another way. A spread of the war might bring in the Super Powers at least indirectly and it would be difficult for us to keep out. We have allies and friends amongst these independent states and we could not simply let them down. Moreover, Chancellor, a war that was extended in time and space would have far more costly effects for us than the preventive action I propose.

PRIME MINISTER. Minister for the Isles.

MINISTER FOR THE ISLES. I think there is a lot of force in what the Foreign Secretary says. My sympathies are with Alcidan. It is in danger of being attacked. If it were provoked into forestalling action, that would not be aggression, but self-defence. We should do all we can to nip aggression by Lorentia in the bud. As the Foreign Secretary has convincingly argued, this would also be in our national interest.

PRIME MINISTER. The Cabinet is clearly very evenly divided. I would like to tell my colleagues my own views. I support the Foreign Secretary. I appreciate what the Secretary of State for

Defence has said and we must take his warnings into account. But I believe we could bring our influence to bear on Lorentia without undue risk. They are a shaky Government, unsure of themselves. They would hesitate to fire on our ships and bring even more trouble upon themselves. Over and above that we will run great political risks if we do not do all we can to protect and rescue British subjects. Another factor weighs heavily with me that has not yet been mentioned. We may be facing a spread of war that would enable Russia to enter this area. America is reluctant to get directly involved—but it would strongly back action by us along the lines suggested by the Foreign Secretary. That is the view of our Ambassador and my own conclusion. We have not had very good relations with America lately. Here we could at one and the same time serve our own interests, get on good terms with the United States and help to keep world peace. I would not consider the American angle if there were not also direct British interests: but it is an extra factor of considerable importance.

I must confess that I am worried about reactions amongst our own people if we do nothing. We have to take some risks for the sake of the great issues at stake. Britain must sometimes stand up. This is a time for stout hearts. I strongly support the Foreign Secretary.

DEFENCE SECRETARY. Prime Minister, to go back to what you said about Lorentia not opening fire on our ships—I did what I was asked to. I examined a particular proposal for action. In my considered view, the military risks are too great to run. I repeat, the Foreign Secretary's proposals would make no military sense. We might assemble a naval force some way off, to bring pressure to bear: but to go into narrow waters in the hope that a wild and inexperienced Government, which has already seized our works, would not open fire—this would expose us to risks against which we could not retaliate.

PRIME MINISTER. Yes, I understood your point. I said we must fully take it into account. Chancellor of the Exchequer.

CHANCELLOR OF THE EXCHEQUER. I don't want to add anything to what I said about the economic and financial aspects. Nothing that has been said has shaken me in my views. On the more general issue I must protest against the tone of some of the remarks made about those of us who do not agree with you and the Foreign Secretary. The Foreign Secretary described us as neutralists. And you, Prime Minister, said that we need stout hearts—implying that those who take a different view are cowards.

PRIME MINISTER. I certainly implied no such thing, Chancellor.

CHANCELLOR OF EXCHEQUER. I'm glad to hear that, Prime Minister. I cast no doubts on the sincerity of anyone who takes a different view from me. I hope my sincerity will be equally acknowledged.

The Foreign Secretary said that there might be a spread of the war and that this might well involve us in still heavier economic cost. Well, Foreign Secretary, like you I have to balance risks. I prefer to be cautious in the beginning—as far as I can see with clarity. I know what the immediate costs of the proposed operation would be. I don't believe the risks of a spread of the war are considerable. Who would want to spread the war? It might spread amongst some of the neighbours of Lorentia and Alcidan— though I don't for the life of me see why. But even if the war spread that far, it wouldn't be a general war. America and Russia might give arms and other aid: but they are not going to risk a direct confrontation.

I have listened very carefully to what you and the Foreign Secretary said—but I think you are both overlooking stubborn facts. We simply have not the resources for that sort of thing. Our first duty is to consider our own national interests. I can't see what national interest compels us to intervene militarily. It certainly wouldn't get us any uranium. Even if you seize and hold the works you can't compel the Lorentians to work. Even if you put in pioneers and kept the works going, you couldn't get uranium from the field: you can't dig uranium with bayonets. Of course the loss of uranium is going to be awkward: but sooner or later Lorentia will have to sell us the uranium again. It's valueless to them without a market: they can't eat uranium. As the Minister of Nuclear Energy said, we must take immediate steps to stop foreign Governments or companies buying our uranium. We must threaten to bring action in the International Court to protect our interests. If America is so keen for us to help them, Prime Minister, we should ask them to join us in keeping other purchasers out, themselves included.

PRIME MINISTER. Minister of Libraries.

MINISTER OF LIBRARIES. Prime Minister, this is perhaps the most serious issue this Cabinet has yet had to face. I agree with the Chancellor of the Exchequer. I think it would be madness to proceed as suggested by the Foreign Secretary. We simply are not concerned. We can no longer take on ourselves an obligation to keep peace everywhere in the world—even in areas where we once had authority. The Foreign Secretary and those who agree with him greatly exaggerate our effectiveness. The Foreign Secretary said that Alcidan wants a guarantee against attack, but it is not *our* guarantee that would satisfy her, only an American guarantee. We must—

PRIME MINISTER. But America won't act and wants us to.

MINISTER OF LIBRARIES. That may well be so, Prime Minister. But that doesn't mean that a guarantee by us would be effective. If America won't or can't act, that clearly means that no military action of any kind is possible and we must think of other means—such as those proposed by the Chancellor. Oh, there was a point I was about to make when you interrupted me, Prime Minister. We must not overlook that if we took military action we would in many countries and almost certainly in the U.N. be branded as an aggressor. We might possibly take the military initiative but would be on the political defensive. The arguments of the Chancellor and the Defence Secretary are very powerful. I think the Foreign Secretary should give his mind to the diplomatic possibilities open to us. I wholeheartedly welcome his proposals about activating the U.N.

PRIME MINISTER. Commonwealth Secretary.

COMMONWEALTH SECRETARY. I agree on the whole with the

Minister of Libraries: indeed his main argument seems to me unanswerable. But I'm not sure about the proposal that we should by ourselves try to activate the United Nations. We are, or appear to be, an interested country. We are always liable to attack for neo-colonialism. We should try to get other nations to take the initiative: we might join in as one of a number of sponsors. We must, too, be careful in which countries we set our Ambassadors to work. Over-eagerness can blow back on us. The final vote could be pretty close. We want every vote that can possibly be got.

PRIME MINISTER. Minister for the Isles.

MINISTER FOR THE ISLES. Prime Minister, I am totally opposed to what the Minister of Libraries said. This is no time for pacifist talk. You can always find reasons for not doing something. We still have some power and influence in the world. Power and influence are there to be used on proper occasions. This is a proper occasion if there ever was one. That other nations want to keep out is all the more reason why we should not. The logical con-clusion of the argument of the Minister of Libraries is that we shouldn't keep any forces at all: that's what follows from his argument that we can't effectively use even a show of force in a relatively minor operation. If you can't use your forces, get rid of them—that's what the Minister of Libraries *should* say.

FOREIGN SECRETARY. Can I come in here again, Prime Minister? I am glad the Minister for the Isles has spoken as he has. It needed saying. The Minister of Libraries has taken a simply defeatist line. Some of my colleagues don't seem able to get it into their heads that it is peace not war that I want. If we don't damp down the fires, there may be a spread of war that would involve us in much worse and—Chancellor—more expensive dangers. I will try and not interrupt too much, Prime Minister—but I feel strongly about this. Some of the things that have been said I deeply resent. They totally misrepresent my policy.

PRIME MINISTER. Don't apologize, Foreign Secretary. I haven't liked all I have heard this morning. Secretary of State for Defence.

DEFENCE SECRETARY. I haven't yet spoken on the merits or rather the demerits of the Foreign Secretary's proposals. Let me say in a word that I agree with the Minister of Libraries that, since we cannot bring effective force to bear, we should not try to.

(Four or five Ministers speak briefly. All but one—who says, 'We can't leave Alcidan in the lurch'—are against military action.)

PRIME MINISTER. Before we come to a conclusion we must consider more closely the safety of our people in Lorentia. One of the main objects of the Foreign Secretary was to put us in a position to rescue our people if necessary. Who would like to speak on this point? Minister of Investment.

MINISTER OF INVESTMENT. I'm glad you've brought us back to this point, Prime Minister. To my mind it is one of the most important of all. If we stand by and do nothing and then British people are killed there will be a public outcry against us and quite right too. If it is found that we can't do anything even after their danger becomes clear, I wouldn't give much for our chances of survival.

PRIME MINISTER. Minister with Portfolio.

MINISTER WITH PORTFOLIO. We've got to keep a sense of proportion. What is military nonsense for one purpose is still military nonsense for another: it's not the objective, but the nature of the operation that matters. If we can't move, we can't move. We would be just as much exposed to political attacks on us for aggression. It would be said that little countries can't rescue their people when in danger in another country: only big countries can do this against little countries.

CHANCELLOR OF THE EXCHEQUER. I have spoken strongly against the Foreign Secretary's proposals. But if the issue is limited to the rescue of British subjects, that's a different matter. There's a strong tradition in this country that if it is at all possible to rescue British subjects we should do so. In spite of what the Minister with Portfolio said, an operation limited to this purpose would, I believe, be understood in the world. Indeed, if we did nothing, we would be condemned.

DEFENCE SECRETARY. I think, Prime Minister, the best thing we could do would be to keep some ships some way off but near enough and in sufficient strength to show that we could act if we were forced to. It would still be dangerous to send ships close inshore. But if one or two ships went in alone with the sole object of getting our people out, I think we could probably get away with it. That would be something openly and palpably different from a military operation. We could allow it to be known that our ships were in the vicinity for this purpose and none other.

MINISTER WITH PORTFOLIO. We must be careful, Prime Minister. We might provoke the very thing we are trying to avoid. Lorentia might be provoked by a show of force into attacking our people.

PRIME MINISTER. Minister of Libraries.

MINISTER OF LIBRARIES. Prime Minister, I too spoke very strongly against the Foreign Secretary's proposals as a whole. I feel equally strongly that the part of the Foreign Secretary's policy that relates to the rescue of our people is right. I don't think there is as much risk as the Minister with Portfolio says: even if there is, we must run it. The risk may not be that the Government of Lorentia will be provoked into attacking British subjects but that it won't be capable of protecting them against public riots and looting. If we make it clear that we are sending ships in and landing men solely to rescue British subjects in imminent danger and are going to withdraw at once—then, as the Chancellor said, our action will be understood. But we must make it clear that our action is limited in this way. I suggest there are two particular steps that we should take. First, make strong and public representations to the Government of Lorentia about the safety of our people and say that we will hold it responsible for anything that happens. Secondly, we should concentrate all British subjects in the compound so that we can reach and rescue them quickly.

(Several Ministers say briefly that they agree.)

PRIME MINISTER. Well, there is a clear preponderance of view in the Cabinet against a military operation. But we are agreed that we must rescue British subjects if they are in danger. This would involve, if necessary, landing men from ships to get our people out and on board. I want the Cabinet to be quite clear about this, as we might have to act at a moment's notice before the Cabinet can be recalled. We will not openly initiate action in the U.N.: but will associate ourselves with any resolution about keeping the peace or accepting a cease fire. We will, with discretion, approach some friendly Governments.

We must urgently approach all countries that have uranium companies to get them to agree not to buy Lorentian uranium so long as our property has been taken without compensation. Lord Chancellor, would you look into the legal position in international law with the Law Officers and the Minister of Nuclear Energy?

LORD CHANCELLOR. Certainly, Prime Minister.

FOREIGN SECRETARY. Have you finished, Prime Minister? Well, I'd like to say this – I agree about the proposals for action in regard to the United Nations. They're too cautious, but it doesn't much matter which way we proceed.

But, Prime Minister, I totally disagree with what you said about no military operation. I am frankly disgusted by the way this discussion has gone. I've never seen such a lack of guts.

PRIME MINISTER. You know I have a good deal of sympathy with your general proposals, Foreign Secretary. But the preponderant view of the Cabinet is clear. We won't get any further by going on any longer.

CHANCELLOR OF THE EXCHEQUER. Could I suggest, Prime Minister, that you set up a working party to go into the effects of the seizure of our works upon our balance of payments. To do this we need to know how much uranium we can still get out, how long Lorentia can hold out and so forth. I think you should send out an emissary to see things on the spot and report back. To the Foreign Secretary let me say that it needs just as much guts in a situation like this to say No as to say Yes.

PRIME MINISTER. I think those are good proposals, Chancellor of the Exchequer. Is the Cabinet agreed with my summing up and the additional points made by the Chancellor?

(Silence, with a few muttered 'Agreeds'.)

Very well. Could you have a word with me, Foreign Secretary, about whom we might send out?

(5) Imaginary Cabinet Meeting (Home Affairs)

PRIME MINISTER. The next item concerns proposals arising out of the Stockington Report. Welfare Minister and Minister of Communications to come in.

(The Assistant Secretary of the Cabinet opens the door. Both Ministers come in, red boxes in hand. The Welfare Minister finds a vacant seat by the Deputy Secretary to the Cabinet: the Minister of Communications sits on a chair against the wall, which he half draws up to the table.)

PRIME MINISTER. Sorry to have kept you both waiting rather long. We have before us a report of the committee I set up under the chairmanship of the President-General. I will ask you to open, President-General, and the Minister of Welfare to follow.

PRESIDENT-GENERAL. Prime Minister, I don't know that I can add much to the paper I have circulated. The proposals of the Welfare Minister consist of three main points. First, that there should be a tax on sweets: secondly, that the advertising of sweets on T.V. should be forbidden and should be restricted in other media: and, thirdly, that free toothbrushes should be issued to children under eleven in the schools—one free brush a year.

As I say in my report, opinion on the committee was very evenly divided. I'm afraid I wasn't able, Prime Minister, to get any acceptable compromise. You've got to accept or reject at any rate proposals one and three—they hold together. You could leave out the proposal on advertising without wrecking the scheme—but it has strong advocates. In the annexe to my report I set out in some detail the technical problems that would be involved by the adoption of the three proposals: none of these would be insoluble. My own view, Prime Minister, tends to favour the proposal. It is a neat one. The revenue from a tax on sweets could be so adjusted that it exactly paid for the cost of the free toothbrushes. This proposal would in a sense cost nothing. The Welfare Minister will speak about the effect on children's health. There is of course also a political angle — I'm inclined to think the proposals would be popular. Certainly the Opposition wouldn't be able to attack them except in detail — because they like this sort of thing. Some of our own fellows will object — most of them, probably, would be opposed in their hearts — but we're getting near enough to an election — whatever date, Prime Minister, you choose — to make attractive any proposal likely to be popular in the country. So, on balance, I support the proposals.

PRIME MINISTER. Minister of Welfare.

WELFARE MINISTER. Prime Minister, I urge these proposals as strongly as I can on my colleagues. I am grateful to the President-General for the way in which he has introduced the papers — but one thing he said I disagree with. The prohibition of T.V. advertising and the restriction on other forms of advertising is essential. After all we are not really concerned with elections, but with the health of our children. This whole thing started with the Stockington Report which showed conclusively the deleterious effect of an excessive sugar-intake on children's teeth and on their health. Those with good teeth grow better, suffer less from illness and even seem to be more intelligent. My three proposals are interlocking and self-balancing. As the President-General has pointed out, the Treasury won't have to pay a penny. If we don't restrict the advertisement of sweets, we might as well drop the whole thing. The sweet manufacturers would simply be undoing the whole point of free toothbrushes. Clearly we can't stop children eating sweets — indeed the Stockington Report shows that, up to a point, this does no harm. It's a sugar-intake over a certain level that causes all the damage. Manufacturers want to get children to eat sugar over the danger level — that's what they're in business for, whatever they may be saying. We want to keep children's teeth safe. Where a private interest is in conflict with a clear public interest it must give way.

Regarding the free toothbrushes, Prime Minister, I know the argument that the Education Secretary is going to use — but there's no alternative to a distribution through teachers in schools. Any arrangement for mothers to get free toothbrushes for their children would be excessively complicated and expensive and, over and above that, full of loopholes for abuse. If it can't be done through the schools, it can't be done at all: and that would be a disaster. The Stockington Report has been very well received in all informed quarters and I have for some time been under pressure in the House to carry it into effect. I don't think I can stall much longer.

I beg my colleagues to agree to a policy that will cost nothing and which will do real good. The policy can be properly administered, as is made clear in the annexe to the paper before us, which was prepared by officials of all the departments concerned.

PRIME MINISTER. Secretary of State for Education, you are much concerned in this.

SECRETARY OF STATE FOR EDUCATION. Yes, Prime Minister, I am. The simple fact is that we cannot put any more chores on the teachers. They are already overloaded. They object to being treated as free labour, doing one service after another for the State, which it ought to pay for itself. The teachers are discontented about their salaries. If we put this extra task upon them we can expect them to press for an earlier increase than the one we must in the normal course expect towards the beginning of next year. Probably they would simply refuse to co-operate. I cannot agree, Prime Minister, to bringing the teachers into this. If the Welfare Minister wants his scheme, he must find another way of carrying it out.

PRIME MINISTER. Chancellor, what have you to say about the fiscal aspect of these proposals?

CHANCELLOR OF THE EXCHEQUER. Well, Prime Minister, let me first deal with the Welfare Minister's point that his proposals would cost nothing. It is true that the proposed tax on sweets could be made to equal the cost of the free toothbrushes. But the free toothbrushes will cost just the same amount, however financed. From the taxpayers' point of view they will be paid for out of extra taxation.

Moreover, Prime Minister, I could never agree to the ear-marking of a tax for a specific expenditure. That is against all our traditions and would be a most dangerous precedent.

Finally, we have before us a proposal to levy a tax. I cannot, as Chancellor of the Exchequer, agree to consider tax proposals apart from my budget. When the time comes I will have to consider my proposals, if any, for tax changes in the light of the general economic situation and of public expenditure as a whole. I can't deal with this proposal in isolation and at this time of the year. I must oppose the proposal.

MINISTER WITH PORTFOLIO. But, Chancellor, this is not a tax in the ordinary sense. Its purpose is to deter an activity that under-mines the health of our children.

CHANCELLOR OF THE EXCHEQUER. Prime Minister, whatever its purpose, it is a tax and therefore falls within my prerogatives as Chancellor.

MINISTER WITH PORTFOLIO. Can I go on, Prime Minister?

(Prime Minister nods.)

The Minister of Welfare's proposal is one of very great social importance. There can be no doubt about the good effect it would have on the health of our children: indeed of a whole generation as the children grow up. If we do nothing, we are making our-selves a party to keeping our children less healthy than they could be. I hope the Chancellor will in these special circumstances re-consider his rather doctrinaire stand. What he says about taxes and budgets may have been all right in Gladstone's time: but we live in different circumstances today.

PRIME MINISTER. Minister for the Isle of Wight.

MINISTER FOR THE ISLE OF WIGHT. I oppose on principle the Chancellor's line. It's time that the Cabinet had the right to discuss, at any rate in broad outline, taxes that the Chancellor might impose or alter. The present method by which the Chancellor tells us of his proposals all together a day or two before the budget deprives the Cabinet of its proper rights: it just sets it aside.

PRIME MINISTER. That's taking us rather far afield. We could perhaps discuss that on another occasion. Let's keep to the issues before us, which are big enough.

MINISTER FOR THE ISLE OF WIGHT. Well, Prime Minister, on the issue immediately before us, I would like to say this. This Government badly needs some measure of social progress. It's this kind of thing that really interests people. And very many people would be interested – not only doctors and nutrition experts but mothers –

(The Education Secretary throws a folded note across the table to the Minister of Investment. 'Dear Bill, Please come in and say a word against this barmy proposal – Christopher.' The Minister of Investment reads the note and nods his head.)

and fathers. Even if teachers don't want to take part, they want healthier children to teach. By the way, although I must defer to the Education Secretary in his own field, don't forget that there was an eminent teacher on the Stockington Commission and I have read letters in the papers from teachers backing the Stockington Report.

SECRETARY OF STATE FOR EDUCATION. I can assure you the teachers as a body won't stand for it.

PRIME MINISTER. Minister of Communications.

MINISTER OF COMMUNICATIONS. Prime Minister, I am sure we'll be in terrible trouble with the television companies if we put a discriminatory restriction upon them. And I must say I think they would be right. Why should we pick on them?

WELFARE MINISTER. That's not true. One of the proposals is to restrict advertising on other media.

MINISTER OF COMMUNICATIONS. First of all, there's a distinction between *banning* advertisements on T.V. and *restricting* them on other media. Secondly, there will be no restriction on other media because we don't want the whole press against us; besides, it would probably push some papers out of circulation. No: in effect the proposal is to pick on television and I think that is wrong.

PRIME MINISTER. Minister of Investment.

MINISTER OF INVESTMENT. I'd like to make two brief points, Prime Minister. First, what does the Minister of Welfare mean when he says he's under parliamentary pressure? It's just a bunch of cranks and interested members who ask questions, quite a lot of them from the other side of the House. We are all under this sort of pressure and we stand up to it. That's one of the things we, including the Welfare Minister, are paid for. The second point is this, we must be careful about pushing people about. I agree there with the Minister of Communications. Who are we to stop people seeing certain sorts of advertisements on T.V. or on the hoardings? If we restrict newspaper advertising we will put some papers into still greater danger. And if people want to eat sweets or want their children to, why on earth should we stop them? We don't want to be a Government of kill-joys. And one other thing—I just don't believe you can stop children eating sweets. To try to is against nature.

CHANCELLOR OF THE EXCHEQUER. Can I come in again, Prime Minister, with just one word. I agree with what has just been said. We must not unnecessarily interfere with people's lives. Let me briefly repeat that I cannot agree to a tax being decided upon in isolation.

PRIME MINISTER. We are getting near one o'clock. I have to see the Ambassador of Neutria then. Can we come to a conclusion?

I think the view of the Cabinet is quite clear. The proposal to stop T.V. advertising is an issue separate from the other two. The general view is that we should drop this proposal.

I agree with the Chancellor that we cannot decide upon a tax before he has considered his budget as a whole: though the discussion we have had has done no harm. We can look at this again when the Chancellor brings his budget proposals before us. If he finds it right to impose a tax on sweets, we can consider the whole matter again. The scheme could, if we wished, be introduced in the next Session. Meanwhile, Minister of Welfare, you will have to resist pressure in the House.

Clearly we cannot impose this extra burden on the teachers.

So if the scheme for free toothbrushes is to work, a new way of administering it must be found.

What I propose is that the matter goes back to the committee. Officials can try and work out an alternative method of administration to be considered by the committee. But the whole thing must depend upon the Chancellor's proposals.

It is vitally important that strict confidence is kept over all this. It would do great harm if it got out that we had been considering such far-reaching proposals. It would make it harder for us to agree on anything if there were leaks. And it would be extremely embarrassing if we decided in the end to do nothing.

Any comments?

Well, then, that finishes the agenda.

PART FOUR

Further Questions

CHAPTER 10

FURTHER QUESTIONS

(1) Wrong Questions

In practical studies it is necessary to put questions that are capable of answer.

About the Cabinet answerless questions are sometimes asked. One example we have already seen in Chapter 8. Another such question has become fashionable, namely—Where does real power lie and what are the actual factors and influences that determine political decisions?

Clearly the Cabinet exists and works in the midst of a complex and interacting social, political and economic environment. Its members individually and collectively are subject to innumerable external and psychological pressures.

But if one seeks to analyse the Cabinet in these terms one gets pushed too far. To the question—What are the factors of ultimate power that move the Cabinet?: the only answer is—Almost everything that happens.

At least three sets of considerations must be taken into account in regard to any important decision. First, psychological and personal: the mood or digestion of a Prime Minister, the rivalry between some members of the Cabinet, the absence of a Minister—these and similar things could matter at a critical moment.

Second, constitutional: the relationship, accepted at a given point in time, between the Prime Minister and other Ministers, between the Cabinet and Parliament and the like could play an important part in some decisions.

Third, political: particular decisions of a Cabinet may be influenced or determined by the representations it receives from vested interests, by reactions in the press, leaks of previous Cabinet discussions, the vigour of the Opposition, splits in the parties, the reports of commissions or of committees of civil servants, the balance of payments, the attitude of foreign powers, the state of public opinion, the course of by-elections, the sitting or the recess of Parliament—and a host of other factors.

A number of specific Cabinet decisions can usefully be probed to a certain depth. But a Cabinet makes many decisions, each one of which may be affected by a mass of things operating in different combinations. If one were to prosecute research into a sufficient range of decisions to justify valid conclusions, one would no longer be analysing the Cabinet but writing a history of the times.

Akin to wrong questions about the Cabinet are comments that presuppose that it is something different from what it can be. For instance the comment that 'the Cabinet does not make policy'; or 'the Cabinet works less satisfactorily ... if it must think for itself or act without a brief.'[1]

The Cabinet is not meant nor designed to do either of these things.

Basically the Cabinet is a constitutional mechanism to ensure that before important decisions are reached many sides of the question are weighed and considered. This means that much work must be done beforehand in interdepartmental discussions and in the preparation of papers for Cabinet Committees and the Cabinet. Cabinets that act without briefs or over-hastily 'think for themselves' usually, in my experience, make mistaken decisions. Political decisions of importance are in their nature complex and need some time and thought. The Cabinet system is extremely well adapted to making considered decisions with all due speed.

The criticism that the Cabinet 'does not make policy' sometimes implies that it does not sufficiently plan ahead.

A number of factors set an upper limit upon the capacity to plan not only under the Cabinet system, but in any advanced country.

Like every other decision-making body, the Cabinet has an immense press of business to attend to. If it is neglected this, the administration of the nation's affairs would suffer and the Cabinet would be rightly blamed for not reaching urgently needed decisions.

As Bagehot observed, 'no policy can get more out of a nation than there is in the nation.'[2] Future policy may depend upon the degree of the propensity of people to save or to consume; upon their dislike of certain changes; upon the mood of workers and business men; and upon similar variables in other countries.

It is impossible to get the up to the minute facts and figures that are needed for confident planning. However much computers and similar devices are used, there must be a time-lag between what is now happening in the economy and the statistical record upon which the planners have to rely. As one Government economic adviser once put it at a meeting of Ministers – The problem is to forecast where we are today.

All attempts at planning encounter another obstacle that is inherent in the nature of things. Planning presupposes the careful co-ordination of policy between those men who have the power to carry the plan into effect. There can be only relatively few such men or administrative confusion would result. Co-ordination of policy consumes much of the time and energy of those few men. Every hour spent on inter-departmental and expert committees must be subtracted from the exiguous ration of hours that a Minister or high civil servant has for the task of administering the plan. Beyond a certain point – the more you plan, the less you execute the plan: the more you execute, the less you plan.

By leadership, policy and administrative skill Governments can, within limits, reduce the checks upon planning of some of these factors. Different systems of government can surmount them in varying degree.

The limit upon planning is perhaps lifted highest under Cabinet government, which is geared and designed for the rapid co-ordination of policy.

The Cabinet system provides for the planning of the legislative programme for the whole life of a Parliament and sometimes for the next Parliament as well: it can secure, through Cabinet Committees, the most detailed consideration of complex social reforms and of economic, financial and military policies. All these can be supervised and co-ordinated by the Cabinet.

To study the Cabinet as such, as I have said, answerable questions must be asked. This I have attempted to do in this book.

The basic question has been—Where does political authority lie? Where can the great political decisions be made?

I hope to have shown that the answer in Britain is—In the Cabinet and in the Cabinet alone. From there one can go on and seek answers to a limited number of related questions. How does the Cabinet proceed to arrive at, register and enforce its decisions? What are its relations with bodies and institutions with which it is in constitutional and regular contact—Crown, Parliament, Party, Opposition, Civil Service?

How far do these factors react upon one another? How far and for what reasons do they change over time?

To such questions meaningful answers can be given, about which there can be meaningful argument.

Since the Cabinet is the seat of political authority, the answers to these questions are of high importance: changes in the Cabinet system are in this country a major means of altering the Constitution.

Some further questions may pertinently be asked about possible future developments in the Cabinet system. These concern changes that may occur in the composition or working of the Cabinet: problems that might arise within the Cabinet structure: consequences of a shift in the basic political forces that brought the present Cabinet system into being.

In the following and concluding pages I discuss some questions of this kind.

(2) Proper Size of Cabinet?

From time to time it is urged that there should be a small Cabinet: and sometimes that it should be composed of non-departmental

Ministers who could devote their whole time to co-ordinating policy.

Such proposals rarely come from Prime Ministers who have had to form a Cabinet. They emanate from commentators or from Leaders of the Opposition who have yet to try their hand at putting an Administration together.

Attlee writing in 1937 maintained that contemporary Cabinets of about twenty-two members were too large. He advocated a Cabinet made up of a 'small group' of Ministers 'in charge of functions not departments'. Departmental Ministers were to be organized in groups outside the Cabinet. Each functional Minister was to be in constant and close contact with a group of departmental Ministers.[3]

Attlee succeeded in keeping his Cabinets down to seventeen or eighteen members; but these Cabinets contained no less than fourteen departmental Ministers. When Churchill introduced Attlee's idea of co-ordinating Ministers in the modified form of the Overlords, he was assailed by Attlee.

Mr Harold Wilson in 1964, before he was in office, regarded the Cabinet of Sir Alec Douglas-Home as 'excessive': it had twenty-three members. He said he had no intention, if he became Prime Minister, of forming a small Cabinet: he wanted a Cabinet between fifteen and twenty-three.[4]

In fact Mr Harold Wilson's Cabinets have contained the 'excessive' number of twenty-three members.

Speaking in the House of Commons on November 21st, 1968, Mr Harold Wilson gave reasons against 'a very much smaller Cabinet either than the present one or the Cabinet of our immediate pre-decessors'. He said he had carefully considered the possibility of 'a Cabinet of, say, eleven or twelve, containing senior Ministers responsible for a wide group of departments'. He rejected this idea on the main grounds that it was similar to the unworkable system of Over-lords: and that 'representative' Ministers could not be left out of the Cabinet. (See Chapter 3, p. 46.)

This speech was in answer to one made by Mr Heath at the Conservative Conference in 1968 in which he went back in part to Lord Attlee's earlier proposals: 'I shall establish a smaller Cabinet as a decision-making body, create federal departments to reduce inter-departmental friction.'

A very small Cabinet, which has been attempted only in wartime, has always been something of a pretence. As we have seen, other Ministers were frequently called in and some were constant attenders.

This would be all the more necessary in peacetime. The Cabinet must co-ordinate and must therefore contain (either formally or in practice) the major departmental Ministers.

A further disadvantage of a small Cabinet of non-departmental Ministers is that these would only rarely appear before Parliament, because they would have no departmental functions for which they were answerable.

The contrary proposition is also advanced that all full Ministers should be brought into the Cabinet. By October 1968, it is argued, the combination of a Cabinet of twenty-three and the amalgamation of a number of departments had the result that only three full Ministers were outside the Cabinet. One of these was the Postmaster General whose office disappeared when the Post Office became a public board. Thus if the Cabinet were enlarged by only two members, all full Ministers would be within it.

But a Cabinet of twenty-five would be far too large – as, indeed, is a Cabinet of twenty-three. Real discussion, co-ordination and decision-making is extremely difficult, if not impossible, in a Cabinet of this size.

A Cabinet larger than seventeen or eighteen ceases to be a council that can easily have a continuous collective view.

It would be wrong either to attempt a very small Cabinet or to enlarge it to include all Ministers. Since a Cabinet today must include three or four Ministers without departmental responsibilities, it would be necessary to return to the practice of Lord Attlee, who in order to keep his Cabinet to reasonable size was prepared to leave a number of Ministers outside it.

One small further step in a well-established direction would be to omit the Lord Chancellor from the Cabinet. The Lord Chancellor has increasingly become the head of a Department of Justice and it would be more appropriate to his functions if he were not a member of a Cabinet of party leaders. If this came about, the Cabinet would normally contain only one peer – the Leader of the House of Lords.

(3) Less Secrecy?

The feeling is widespread that the Cabinet shrouds its affairs in too much secrecy and that Parliament, press and public should be able to participate to a greater degree in the formulation of policy.

We must be clear what is at issue. Neither Cabinet decisions nor Cabinet discussions could be more fully disclosed.

With few exceptions Cabinet *decisions* have to be made public in order to be made effective. Only a small number that do not need to be executed do not become known – for instance talks with a foreign country or a decision not to take some action.

All other Cabinet decisions are necessarily disclosed and are subject to public scrutiny and criticism. They may in consequence be modified: some examples were given in Chapter 4, p. 64. Another example (which I consider below) was the decision taken in 1967 about the location of the third London airport.

Cabinet *discussions* as distinct from Cabinet decisions must, from their nature, be kept secret.

Members of the Cabinet, as party leaders, cannot differ from one another in public unless the whole Cabinet system is altered. During discussions leading up to a decision, the members of a Cabinet ought often to differ. Official disclosure of Cabinet discussions would not only reveal these differences but tend to draw Ministers into public participation in them.

A point of quite a different kind is that Cabinet discussions often depend upon confidential advice from civil servants or reports from Ambassadors. If those were disclosed and thus became subject to public attack, it would be extremely difficult for the Cabinet to secure free and frank advice.

Somewhat the same considerations apply to consultations between the Cabinet and outside interests – such as the Trades Union Congress and the Confederation of British Industries. Cabinet discussions might well involve the secrets of these bodies as well as those of the Cabinet. In any case, if Cabinet discussions were disclosed, there would be no possibility of confidential advice from interested bodies: it would always have to be given in public and out loud.

As we have seen in Chapter 2, pp. 30–34, the secrecy surrounding Cabinet discussions is somewhat mitigated by official guidance to the press from No. 10 and by unattributable Ministerial leaks.

This is as far as the disclosure of Cabinet discussions can go. Public argument can take place on the basis of unofficial press guesswork: but any more official disclosure before an actual Cabinet decision is made public would impair the capacity to make decisions.

The main effective change towards less secrecy would be for the Cabinet to share with Parliament and public more of the factual information on which the Government make some of their decisions. Moves in this direction have begun to be taken.

The decision about Stansted airport is an example of a new technique that was worked out, partly due to lively public discussion, for dealing with complex planning problems.

The reason why in this case the question came before the Cabinet when it did was because, up until that time, public inquiry into planning questions was limited by law to *local* planning projects. No method was available for public inquiry into undertakings of national importance involving assessment and comparison of alternatives in a number of different areas.

In fact proposed legislation to provide for public inquiries into national planning projects was being considered in a Cabinet Committee. The question was a complex one involving rights of appeal and the like, and prolonged talks with local authorities. No decision had been reached when it became clear that foreseeable overcrowding of London's two existing airports made it urgent to consider where to place a third one.

The matter therefore came before the Cabinet in 1967 because there was no other machinery for preparatory investigation of such a question.

The Cabinet found it very hard to reach a decision and considered the matter at length at three or four meetings. The conclusion was a reluctant one forced upon Ministers by what appeared to be unanswerable arguments.

Publication of the decision to locate the third London airport at Stansted evoked considerable public concern and controversy. The Cabinet then discussed the issue again and amended its original decision in regard to the siting of runways.

The necessary Order was passed by the House of Commons; but the Cabinet became aware that it might be rejected in the Lords. Rejection of an Order by the Lords was extremely rare and, normally, would have caused no concern: it could easily be put right by another vote in the Commons. On this occasion public opinion seemed to be stirred to a point that would make difficult a reversal of the Lords' rejection of the Order.

By this time the Cabinet had approved the committee's proposals for legislation to set up a new system of inquiry into planning projects on a national scale. Much time would be needed to pass the new scheme into law. So the Cabinet decided to set up an ad hoc commission of inquiry into the third London airport of the kind that would be provided for when the proposed legislation became law.

The ultimate decision to be submitted to Parliament must remain with the Cabinet. It is the seat of political authority and a matter of such high importance could not be settled anywhere else. The decision could not be left to the commission of inquiry, for that would entail conceding to it the power to determine public expenditure. One of the major factors in the problem was the comparative cost of different alternatives.

The removal from the Cabinet of the preparatory stages of certain discussions, to which it is by its nature not apt, could profitably be extended.

The device of the Green Paper enables Parliament and public to make their views known between the initial Cabinet discussions and the final decision. A Green Paper differs from a White Paper which embodies settled Government policy. A Green Paper sets out tentative ideas and invites public discussion on them. The first Green Paper — 'A Proposal for a Regional Employment Premium' — was issued in 1967. Two more — 'The Administrative Structure of the Medical and related Services in England and Wales' and 'How fast?' (Ministry of Transport) — appeared in 1968. A fourth Green Paper — 'The Task Ahead' — came out in 1969. All were published by the Stationery Office.

The discussions in the Cabinet leading up to the publication of a Green Paper as well as those before a final decision must be secret. But this final decision may well be influenced and affected by public participation in the debate between the two sets of Cabinet discussion. In February 1969 Mr Crossman, Secretary of State for Social Services, withdrew the Green Paper on the structure of the Medical Services for reconsideration in the light of its public reception.

Quite apart from Cabinet discussions is the question of the secrecy surrounding established departmental policies and activities. The setting up of a new kind of House of Commons select committee has widened parliamentary inquiry into this field. Each of these select committees investigates for two or three years some aspect of a given department's work. The first, the Select Committee on Science and Technology, was set up in January 1967. The Select Committee on Agriculture was appointed in December 1967: and the Select Committee on Education and Science, in February 1968.

These committees bear a superficial resemblance to the standing committees in continental Parliaments which inquire into subjects such as foreign, commercial, agricultural policy and the like. In fact the House of Commons committees have adapted themselves to the traditional British parliamentary pattern and have developed along different lines.

They have not, like the continental committees, become independent and jealous bodies asserting the right to first information and prior discussion on all important matters in their field of competence.

This would appear to British eyes as a usurpation of the functions and rights of the House as a whole. The select committees act on behalf of the House, but only in specified and limited fields (which they choose for themselves): normally they sit in public and submit written reports to the House as they go along.

These select committees have done useful work in removing an unnecessary veil from sectors of Government policy. In matters of security and special secrecy or in matters that affect private interests, they exclude the public from their sittings and co-operate with the department concerned in suppressing certain passages in their reports to the House.

This development in parliamentary procedure could be carried further. For instance, the Foreign and Commonwealth Office should, for a period, be subjected to investigation by a select committee. In all fields of policy a Cabinet needs the backing of an informed public opinion, but particularly so in foreign policy, which has too long and too impenetrably been wrapped in secrecy.

(4) Could a Prime Minister be removed?

A Prime Minister with his pre-eminence and his distinctive rights was by the 1950s and 1960s in a very secure position, capable of weathering political storms and attacks upon him from within and outside his party. It cannot, however, be excluded that a Prime Minister might be challenged and deposed. No Prime Minister can ignore the possibility of revolt or intrigue in his parliamentary party succeeding.[5] The political precondition for such an event would be very widespread feeling amongst members of his parliamentary party that under the Prime Minister they would have little or no hope of winning the next general election and that the chances would be greatly improved under another leader.

Whether or not the removal of a Prime Minister should prove at any time feasible, the mechanism by which it could come about can be imagined.

A Prime Minister could be overthrown by a revolt of his Cabinet. As we saw (in Chapter 5), this is what happened to Gladstone in 1894, to Asquith in 1916 and to Ramsay MacDonald in 1931. On the other hand when Lloyd George was deposed he had his Cabinet with him, but lost his majority in Parliament.

A second possibility would be a move in the parliamentary party. The power of this body has in some respects grown with that of the Prime Minister. Election as leader by the parliamentary party is the indispensable route to the office of Prime Minister: continuing support in the party is the precondition of the Prime Minister's authority in Parliament. Today Baldwin would have had to face a meeting of Conservative M.P.s instead of, as in 1930, a meeting of M.P.s, peers and parliamentary candidates.

The right of the parliamentary party to select a leader implies the right to choose a new leader in place of a Prime Minister who has lost the confidence of the party. A strong request for a meeting to consider the leadership could not be refused any more than Baldwin was able to refuse it.

One matter that would, in such a case, have to be settled and which could possibly influence the outcome, would be whether the voting should be by ballot or by show of hands. In both parties the original election of a leader is by secret ballot: it would seem logical that a vote about the continuance in office or the removal of a leader should be taken in the same manner.

Should a Prime Minister ever be overthrown in such a way, the question might arise whether he would still have the right to a dissolution of Parliament.

In any matter of this kind, it is essential that the Crown should not be faced with a choice: for then the Crown could be blamed whatever the action taken.

The right to decide on a dissolution of Parliament passed from the Cabinet to the Prime Minister after the first world war. But the right inheres in the Prime Minister as such.

What, then, is a Prime Minister? He has a number of capacities, but chief amongst them is the command of both Cabinet and Parliament. On this depends his right to a dissolution. A Prime Minister who has been overthrown either by his Cabinet or by a vote of the parliamentary party or by both ceases to be a Prime Minister, save in the most formal sense; and cannot therefore advise the Crown.

If Lloyd George had asked for a dissolution before it was known that the Carlton Club meeting was to be held, then the Crown would have had to accept his advice: for he would still have been Prime Minister in fact as well as title. If he had asked for a dissolution after the meeting had been convened or after it had voted, the Crown could not have accepted the advice, because it would no longer have been tendered by a real Prime Minister.

This is not, therefore, a matter for the discretion of the Crown. If advice to dissolve in these circumstances were accepted, the Crown would be interfering in the internal affairs of a party—and the majority party at that. Since the Crown must keep clear of party politics, it has only one course. Once a party meeting has been called for in order to consider the question of leadership, no advice to dissolve is valid until there is a Prime Minister in the full sense of the word.

Should a Prime Minister be removed, the parliamentary party would (as in the case of his death or resignation) have to go into immediate and continued session to elect his successor.

The Crown must await the decision of this meeting of the parliamentary party. Whatever its outcome—the vindication of the Prime Minister or the election of a new party leader—there would again be a Prime Minister in the full sense of the word. If this Prime Minister should still wish for a dissolution, then the Crown would have to accept his advice.

(5) Break-up of Two-party System?

The evolution of the Cabinet of the 1950s and 1960s was fundamentally due to the establishment of a stable mass two-party system.

The two-party system broke down on occasion in the nineteenth century and the first quarter of the twentieth. But the forces making for a two-party system grew stronger and more persistent during the course of the last hundred years and the two-party system became very stable from the second world war onwards.

It is conceivable that it might collapse. Each of the two parties is,

and must be, a coalition: and each could therefore in certain circumstances split. One or more nationalist parties might arise and maintain
a number of members in Parliament. As in Gladstone's day, one of the
two major parties might, in the search for a majority, come to a political arrangement with a nationalist party: as in Gladstone's day, it
might split in consequence.

What would be the probable effects of a breakdown of the two-party
system?

At best a victorious party in a general election would emerge with a
small or very small majority.

Party discipline in Parliament would become stricter and the
tolerance allowed to dissenters in the 1950s and 1960s would be eclipsed.
A Government in office would need all its votes to keep it there until
at least a favourable moment occurred for a new general election. The
other parties would need all their votes in order to manœuvre and
take advantage of a critical situation.

The Cabinet would continue to function in the same way, but it
would lack the self-confidence and assurance of a certain life-span that
Cabinets of the 1950s and 1960s had acquired.

It might well be that on occasion no party would receive a clear
majority in an election. There might therefore be more than one
possible Prime Minister at the beginning of a Parliament or during its
course if a combination of other parties overthrew the Government
and brought about a new, perhaps not very stable, majority in Parliament.

Would in these circumstances the Crown reacquire the right to
'choose' a Prime Minister?

The duty of the Monarch to avoid involvement in party politics
would mean that the Crown should exercise no initiative whatever.
If the impression arose that it was trying to give one party an advantage,
it would be in danger of being attacked by all the others.

And to no purpose. As we have seen, even Queen Victoria had only
an apparent and not a real power to choose a Prime Minister: the
actual decision was made by the party leaders.

The only course open to the Crown would be to await the outcome of negotiations between the party leaders. Since these would have the effective decision in their hands, the duty would lie on them to agree speedily upon a leader for whom the Queen could send.

Even should they not quickly resolve their problem, it would still remain the constitutional obligation not of the Crown but of the political leaders to find the way out. If blame there is to be, it must fall on political leaders. The Crown must be and remain beyond criticism.

The same basic forces would continue to operate which by the 1950s and 1960s had created a strong tendency towards a stable mass two-party system.

In all probability political instability would result in fairly frequent general elections. It would become apparent that no party and no body of electors could secure the execution of any steady policy or programme of legislation.

The desire of parties and people to get possession of the Cabinet for at least the duration of a Parliament would work against the long continuance of a multi-party system. After perhaps some realignment of the parties, the re-establishment would be highly probable of a stable mass two-party system, which is the basis of modern British Cabinet government.

Committee Name	Pre-1914	1914–18	1918–40	1940–54
War	× (2)	—	—	—
National Defence	× (2)	—	—	—
Imperial Defence	× ★(3)	—	× ★	—
War	—	× ★(4)	—	—
Dardanelles	—	× ★(5)	—	—
Defence (Operations)	—	—	—	× ★
Defence (Supply)	—	—	—	× ★
Defence	—	—	—	—
Economic Defence and Development	—	—	× ★	—
Post-war Priority	—	—	×	—
Finance	—	—	× (7)	—
Irish Situation	—	—	× (7)	—
Iron and Steel	—	—	× (7)	—
House of Lords Reform	—	—	× (7)	—
Pub. of Secret Documents	—	—	× (7)	—
Economy	—	—	× (8)	—
Economic Policy	—	—	—	× †
Home Affairs	—	—	×	—
Lord President's	—	—	—	× †
Reconstruction	—	—	—	× †
Food Policy	—	—	—	× †
Civil Defence	—	—	—	× †
Colonial ⎫	—	—	—	—
India ⎬	—	—	—	—
Commonwealth	—	—	—	—
Future Legislation	—	—	—	—
Legislation	—	—	—	—
Machinery of Government and Information Services	—	—	—	—
Manpower	—	—	—	—
Socialization of Industry	—	—	—	—
China and South-east Asia	—	—	—	—
Middle East	—	—	—	—
Civil Aviation	—	—	—	—
Social Services	—	—	—	—
Production	—	—	—	—
Atomic Energy	—	—	—	—
Foreign Affairs	—	—	—	—
Overseas Policy and Defence	—	—	—	—
Agricultural Policy	—	—	×	—
Nuclear Defence	—	—	—	—
Public Expenditure	—	—	—	—
Public Expenditure Scrutiny	—	—	—	—
Prices and Incomes	—	—	—	—

NOTES

1. Divisions after 1940 are made at the start of new Governments. The one exception is 1947 when it is known that Attlee reconstructed the committee structure.
2. Created 1858; dissolved 1888, when the National Defence Committee was created.
3. Created 1902 from the National Defence Committee.
4. Not to be confused with the later War *Cabinet*.
5. Created in 1915 out of the War Committee.
6. Merged with the Foreign Affairs Committee in 1963 to form the Overseas Policy and Defence Committee.
7. These committees existed during the period 1916–25. Exact dates are not clear.

945-7	1947-51	1951-5	1955-7	1957-63	1963-4	1964
—	—	—	—	—	—	—
—	—	—	—	—	—	—
—	—	—	—	—	—	—
—	—	—	—	—	—	—
—	—	—	—	—	—	—
—	—	—	—	—	—	—
—	—	—	—	—	—	—
—	—	—	—	—	—	—
†	× †	× ★	× ★	× ★	× ★(6)	× ★
—	—	—	—	—	—	—
—	—	—	—	—	—	—
—	—	—	—	—	—	—
—	—	—	—	—	—	—
—	—	—	—	—	—	—
—	—	—	—	—	—	—
—	—	—	—	—	—	—
—	—	—	—	—	—	—
★	× ★	× †	× †	× †	× †	× ★
× †	× †	× †	× †	× †	× †	× †
†	—	—	—	—	—	
†	—	—	—	—	—	
†	× †					—
†	—	—	—	—	—	
★	—	—	—	—	—	
×	× ★	×	×	×	×	× ★
†	× †	× †	× †	× †	× †	× †
†	× †	× †	× †	× †	× †	× †
†	× †					—
†	× †					—
†	× †	—	—	—	—	—
★	× ★					—
†	× †					—
†	× †					—
—	× †					× †
—	× †					× †
—	—	× †	× †	× †	—	—
—	—	× †	× ★(10)	× ★	× ★(6)	—
—	—	—	—	—	× ★	× ★
—	—	—	—			× †
—	—	—	—			× †
—	—	—	× (11)	×		× †(12)
—	—	—	—	×		× †(12)
—	—	—	—	—	—	× †

8. Created 1931. Met infrequently.
9. Created 1944.
10. Created 1956.
11. Created 1961.
12. Became Public Expenditure Scrutiny Committee in 1965.

★ Chaired by Prime Minister
† Chaired by other Cabinet Minister

Although every effort has been made to make this table as complete as possible, it is clear that the portrayal of the committee structure between 1951 and 1964 is not complete.

NOTES

(For fuller particulars see 'List of Books Cited in the Text' p. 183)

CHAPTER I

[1] Crossman, p. 51.
[2] Mackintosh, p. 529.
[3] Bagehot, p. 162.
[4] Campion, p. 14.
[5] Crossman, pp. 48, 51-2.
[6] Campion, p. 65.
[7] Ilbert, p. xiv.
[8] Ilbert, p. xiv.
[9] Campion, p. 23.
[10] Duverger, p. 218 n.
[11] Michels, passim.
[12] Neustadt, pp. 33-4, 187.
[13] Butler, p. 5.
[14] Mackintosh, p. 177.
[15] Ostrogorski, p. 205.
[16] Redlich, i, p. 120.
[17] Ostrogorski, p. 214.
[18] Mackintosh, pp. 259, 266 n.
[19] Campion, p. 23.
[20] Redlich, ii, p. 135.
[21] Mackintosh, p. 209.
[22] Redlich, i, pp. 194-5.
[23] Mackintosh, pp. 124, 138-40.
[24] Bagehot, p. 102.
[25] Ostrogorski, p. 175; Mackenzie, p. 12.
[26] Ostrogorski, pp. 308-9.
[27] Mackenzie, pp. 166, 170.
[28] Mackenzie, pp. 202, 204.
[29] Overacker, pp. 76-9.
[30] Mackenzie, pp. 297, 301, 410.
[31] Asquith, ii, p. 170.

CHAPTER 2

[1] Mackintosh, pp. 142-3; Jennings, pp. 261-2.
[2] Mackintosh, p. 318; Jennings, p. 262.
[3] Asquith, ii, p. 196.
[4] Mackintosh, p. 318-19.
[5] Jones, *Diary*, i, pp. 170, 180.
[6] Amery, p. 73.
[7] Mackintosh, p. 411.
[8] Mackintosh, p. 265-6.
[9] Mackesey, p. 22-3.
[10] Harcourt, p. 610.
[11] Mackintosh, p. 266.
[12] Haldane, p. 216-17.
[13] Harcourt, p. 610.
[14] Monypenny & Buckle, i, p. 1599.
[15] Mackintosh, p.100 n.
[16] Balfour, p. 131.
[17] Mackintosh, p. 226.
[18] Jones, *Diary*, i, p. 227 (note by editor).
[19] Mackintosh, pp. 301-2.
[20] Mackintosh, pp. 70, 301; Jennings, p. 229.
[21] Daalder, p. 53; Jennings, p. 300; Jones, p. 96.
[22] Daalder, p. 56.
[23] Williams, p. 45.
[24] Mackintosh, p. 303.
[25] Gilmour, p. 221.
[26] Jennings, p. 249; Daalder, p. 244.

CHAPTER 3

[1] Gilmour, p. 228.
[2] Webb, p. 38; Snowden, ii, pp. 924-5; Mackintosh, pp. 472-5.
[3] Mackintosh, p. 148; Jennings, p. 253.
[4] Mackintosh, p. 263.

Notes

CHAPTER 3 (*Cont.*)

[5] Hankey, *Supreme Command*, i, pp. 226–7.
[6] Jones, *Diary*, i, p. 123.
[7] Jennings, p. 255; Jones, *Diary*, i, pp. 123, 162, 185, 233, 264, 311, 331.
[8] Daaldar, p. 245.
[9] Daalder, p. 68; Jennings, p. 142.
[10] Mackintosh, p. 512.
[11] Mackintosh, p. 503.
[12] Dalton, p. 195.
[13] Daalder, pp. 110–18.
[14] Gilmour, p. 231.
[15] Crossman, p. 49.
[16] Mackenzie & Grove, p. 339.

[17] Jennings, p. 243.
[18] Daalder, pp. 30, 49.
[19] Daalder, p. 49; Mackintosh, p. 392.
[20] Jones, *Diary*, i, p. 218.
[21] Hankey, *Diplomacy*, pp. 47–52.
[22] Daalder, p. 60; Mackintosh, p. 392; Jennings, p. 244; Jones, *Diary*, i, pp. 123–4, 202, 291–2.
[23] Jones, *Diary* i, p. 250.
[24] Mackenzie & Grove, p. 341.
[25] Jones, *Diary*, i, p. 72.
[26] 'Whitehall and Beyond', p. 28.
[27] Daalder, p. 245.

CHAPTER 4

[1] Daalder, p. 4.
[2] Campion, p. 27.
[3] Bagehot, pp. 154–5.
[4] Rose, p. 194.
[5] Mackintosh, p. 270.
[6] Gardiner, ii, ch. 16.
[7] Mackintosh, pp. 164, 324.
[8] Jenkins, p. 196.
[9] Dalton, p. 25.
[10] Mackintosh, pp. 27–8.
[11] Bagehot, pp. 134, 224.
[12] Mackintosh, p. 101.
[13] Mackintosh, p. 292; Potter, pp. 32, 229.
[14] Mackintosh, p. 10.
[15] Mackenzie & Grove, p. 460.
[16] Potter, p. 291.
[17] Mackintosh, p. 214.
[18] Mackintosh, p. 580.
[19] Mackintosh, p. 584.
[20] Gilmour, p. 11.

[21] Daalder, p. 242.
[22] Mackenzie & Grove, p. 449.
[23] Mackintosh, p. 287.
[24] Parly. Comm. 4th Report, 1967–8.
[25] Sel. Cttee. on Parly. Comm., 1968.
[26] Parly. Comm. 1st Report 1968–9.
[27] Bagehot, ch. 2.
[28] Jennings, pp. 330, 402.
[29] Bagehot, pp. 94, 99, 111.
[30] Harcourt, p. 611.
[31] Jennings, pp. 44–5.
[32] Daalder, p. 99.
[33] Nicolson, pp. 201, 226.
[34] Jennings, p. 413.
[35] Jennings, pp. 415, 423.
[36] Jennings, p. 426.
[37] Jennings, pp. 411–12.
[38] Nicolson, p. 223.
[39] Jennings, p. 397.
[40] Mackintosh, p. 136.

CHAPTER 5

[1] Bagehot, p. 266 n; Jenkins, p. 185.
[2] Hankey, *Diplomacy*, p. 49.
[3] Mackesey, p. 182.
[4] Mackintosh, p. 158 n.
[5] Mackintosh, p. 315; Magnus, p. 418.
[6] Jones, *Diary*, i, pp. 54, 306.
[7] Mackintosh. p. 300.
[8] Daalder, p. 62.

[9] Jennings, pp. 69–70.
[10] Harcourt, p. 611.
[11] Mackintosh, p. 312.
[12] Jennings, p. 417; Magnus, p. 414; Mackintosh, pp. 191–2; Asquith, ii, p. 195.
[13] Asquith, ii, p. 195; Jennings, p. 417.
[14] Jennings, p. 418.

Notes

[15] Blake, p. 385.
[16] Jennings, p. 419.
[17] Mackintosh, p. 449.
[18] Clynes, ii, p. 63.
[19] Mackintosh, p. 317.
[20] Crossman, pp. 48–52.
[21] Mackintosh, p. 389.
[22] Gilmour, p. 206.
[23] Mackintosh, p. 309; Magnus, p. 299.
[24] Gilmour, p. 207.
[25] Balfour, p. 131.
[26] Jennings, p. 188.
[27] Gilmour, pp. 226–7.
[28] Jennings, p. 223.
[29] Haldane, p. 329.
[30] Feiling, p. 363; Jennings, p. 242.
[31] Haldane, p. 329.
[32] Mackintosh, p. 331.
[33] Jones, *Diary*, i, p. 111.

[34] Mackintosh, pp. 334–43; Jones, *Diary*, i, p. 111.
[35] Mackintosh, p. 341.
[36] Crossman, p. 50.
[37] Mackintosh, pp. 25–7; pp. 500–01.
[38] Magnus, p. 169; Asquith, ii, p. 193.
[39] Mackenzie, p. 303.
[40] Mackintosh, pp. 376, 386.
[41] Mackintosh, p. 390; Jones, *Diary*, i, p. 163.
[42] Mackintosh, p. 469; Jones, *Diary*, i, pp. 225–8, 242.
[43] Gilmour, p. 207.
[44] Mackintosh, pp. 499–500.
[45] Daalder, p. 54.
[46] Mackintosh, p. 397.
[47] Mackenzie, p. 131.
[48] Gilmour, p. 219.
[49] Churchill, iii, p. 392.

CHAPTER 6

[1] Hankey, *Diplomacy*, p. 47; Mackintosh, p. 158.
[2] Gilmour, p. 221.
[3] Redlich, i, p. 158.
[4] Mackintosh, pp. 305, 383–4; Jones, *Diary*, pp. 157, 169–70, 178–80, 197.
[5] Mackintosh, p. 305 n.
[6] Mackintosh, p. 305.
[7] Churchill, iii, p. 392.
[8] Morrison, p. 10.
[9] Mackintosh, p. 305.

[10] Asquith, i, p. 196; Mackintosh, p. 391; Daalder, p. 65; Jones, *Diary*, i, pp. 124, 157, 193.
[11] Mackintosh, p. 166.
[12] Jennings, p. 250; Jones, *Diary*, i, p. 251.
[13] Jones, *Diary*, p. 251.
[14] Gilmour, p. 222.
[15] Mackintosh, p. 166.
[16] Macmillan, p. 486.
[17] Macmillan, p. 487.

CHAPTER 7

[1] Jones, *Diary*, i, p. 202.

CHAPTER 10

[1] Mackintosh, pp. 483, 464 (1962 ed.; omitted in 1968 ed.).
[2] Bagehot, p. 206.

[3] Attlee, pp. 173–5.
[4] 'Whitehall and Beyond'.
[5] Gilmour, p. 216.

LIST OF BOOKS CITED IN THE TEXT

AS CITED   FULLER PARTICULARS

Amery   Amery, L. S., *Thoughts on the Constitution* (London, Oxford University Press, 1947)

Asquith   Asquith, H., *Fifty Years of Parliament* (London, Cassell & Co., 1926)

Attlee   Attlee, C. R., *The Labour Party in Perspective* (London, Victor Gollancz, 1937)

Bagehot   Bagehot, Walter, *The English Constitution* (new ed. London, Collins, 1963)

Balfour   Balfour, A. J., *Chapters of Autobiography* (London, Cassell & Co, 1930)

Blake   Blake, Robert, *The Unknown Prime Minister* (London, Eyre & Spottiswoode, 1955)

Butler   Butler, D. E., *The Electoral System in Britain 1918–51* (Oxford, Clarendon Press, 1953)

Campion   Campion, Lord, L. S. Amery and others, *Parliament: a Survey* (London, George Allen & Unwin, 1952)

Churchill   Churchill, Sir W., *The Second World War* (London, Educational Book Co., 1955)

Clynes   Clynes, J. R., *Memoirs* (London, Hutchinson & Co., 1937)

Crossman   Crossman, R. H. S., 'Introduction to Bagehot' (see above)

Daalder   Daalder, Hans, *Cabinet Reform in Britain 1914–63* (London, Oxford University Press, 1964)

Dalton   Dalton, Hugh, *High Tide and After: Memoirs 1945–60* (London, Frederick Muller, 1962)

Duverger   Duverger, Maurice, *Political Parties* (London, Methuen & Co., 1959)

Feiling   Feiling, Keith, *Life of Neville Chamberlain* (London, Macmillan & Co., 1946)

Gardiner   Gardiner, A. R., *William Harcourt* (London, Constable & Co., 1923)

Gilmour   Gilmour, Ian, *The Body Politic* (London, Hutchinson & Co., 1969)

Haldane   Haldane, R. B., *An Autobiography* (London, Hodder & Stoughton, 1929)

List of Books Cited in the Text

Hankey, Hankey, Lord, *Diplomacy by Conference* (London, Ernest
 Diplomacy Benn, 1946)

Hankey, Hankey, Lord, *The Supreme Command 1914–1918* (London,
 Supreme George Allen & Unwin, 1961)
 Command

Harcourt Harcourt, W., Memorandum, in Gardiner at p. 111 (see
 above)

Ilbert . Ilbert, Courtenay, introductory chapter to Redlich (see
 below)

Jenkins Jenkins, Roy, *Asquith* (London, Collins, 1964)

Jennings Jennings, Sir I., *Cabinet Government* (ed.) (Cambridge,
 University Press, 1959)

Jones Jones, T., *Lloyd George* (London, University Press, 1951)

Jones, *Diary* Jones, T., *Whitehall Diary*, vol. i (London, Oxford University Press, 1969)

Mackenzie Mackenzie, R. T., *British Political Parties* (London, William
 Heinemann, 1955)

Mackenzie Mackenzie, W. J. M. and Grove, J. W., *Central Adminis-*
 & Grove *tration in Britain* (London, Longmans, Green & Co., 1957)

Mackesey Mackesey, Piers, *The War for America 1775–83* (London,
 Longmans & Co., 1964)

Mackintosh Mackintosh, John P., *The British Cabinet* (2nd ed. 1968)

Macmillan Macmillan, Harold, *Tides of Fortune* (London, Macmillan
 & Co., 1969)

Magnus Magnus, P., *Gladstone: a Biography* (London, John Murray,
 1954)

Michels Michels, Robert, *Parties* (London, Jarrold & Sons, 1915)

Monypenny Monypenny, W. F. and Buckle, G. E., *Life of Benjamin*
 & Buckle *Disraeli* (London, John Murray, 1929 ed.)

Morrison Morrison, Herbert, *Government and Parliament* (London,
 Oxford University Press, 1954)

Neustadt Neustadt, Richard E., *Presidential Power* (London, John
 Wiley & Sons, 1960)

Nicolson Nicolson, Harold, *King George V* (London, Constable &
 Co., 1952)

Ostrogorski Ostrogorski, M., *Democracy and the Organization of Political*
 Parties (London, Macmillan & Co., 1902)

Overacker Overacker, L., *The Australian Party System* (New Haven,
 Yale University Press, 1952)

Parly. Comm. *Fourth Report of the Parliamentary Commissioner for Adminis-*
 4th Report *tration. Annual Report for 1967* (Feb. 1968)

List of Books Cited in the Text

Parly. Comm.   *First Report of the Parliamentary Commissioner for Adminis-*
  1st Report   *tration. Session 1968–9* (Nov. 1968)

Potter   Potter, Allen, *Organized Groups in British National Politics*
                (London, Faber & Faber, 1961)

Redlich   Redlich, Josef, *The Procedure of the House of Commons*
                (London, Archibald Constable & Co., 1908)

Rose   Rose, R., *Politics in England* (London, Faber & Faber, 1965)

Sel. Cttee. on   *Select Committee on the Parliamentary Commissioner for Ad-*
  Parly. Comm. *ministration. Session 1967–8* (July, 1968).

Snowden   Snowden, Philip, *Autobiography* (London, Nicolson &
                Watson, 1934)

Webb   Webb, Beatrice, *Diaries 1912–24* (ed. M. I. Cole) (London
                Longmans, Green & Co., 1956)

'Whitehall   B.B.C. Publication 1964
  & Beyond'

Williams   Williams, Francis, *The Triple Challenge* (London, William
                Heinemann, 1948)

INDEX

187

Index

Congress of Berlin, 83
Conservative National Union, 18, 21
Conservative Party, 18, 21, 65, 75
Conservative Party Conference, 22
Cooper, A. Duff, 91
Co-ordination of Departments, 28–30
Corrupt Practices Act (1883), 17
Creech-Jones, Arthur, 135–6
Crichel Down, 69
Cripps, Sir Stafford, 40, 120, 135–6
Crossman, R. H. S., 13–14, 45, 47, 85–6, 89, 170
Crown, the, powers of, 71–9, 174–5
Curzon, Lord, 73, 92, 93, 100
Czechoslovakia, Russian invasion of, 96, 117

Daily Mirror, 85
Dalton, Hugh, 29, 60, 105
Defence, Ministry of, 36, 38
Defence Committee, 43, 44
Defence White Papers, 117, 125, 126–30
Derby, Lord, 20, 31, 82, 105
Devaluation (1967), 116, 129
Dilke, Sir Charles, 88
Dillon, John, 27
Disraeli, Benjamin, 18, 29, 62, 81, 82, 83, 87, 105
Diversion of Shipping Committee, 41
Douglas-Home, Sir Alec, 74, 95, 165
Downing Street, Number Ten, 32, 80, 99–106, 110–11
Dugdale, Sir Thomas, 69

ECONOMIC PLANNING COMMITTEE, 43, 45
Economic Policy Committee (1942), 42, 43, 44
Economy Committee, 41
Eden, Anthony, 28, 40, 83, 86–8, 89, 92, 110
Education, Board of, 35; Minister of, 37
Education Bill (1902), 27; (1944), 42–3
Edward VII, 41
Elizabeth II, 74
Evatt, Herbert, 135–6

FARM PRICE REVIEW, 43, 44, 117
Food, Ministry of, 62
Food Policy Committee (1942), 42

Foreign and Commonwealth Affairs 115–16
Foreign Office telegrams, 88
Frequency of Cabinet Meetings, 38
Future Legislation Committee, 43

GAITSKELL, HUGH, 24, 60, 135
Geddes, Eric, 39
George III, 30, 50
George V, 72, 73, 74, 75–8, 84
Gladstone, W. E., 15, 20–21, 27, 29, 36, 59, 62, 73, 81, 82, 83, 86–7, 91–3, 99, 107–8, 109, 171–2, 174
Gordon Walker, Patrick, 29, 40, 44, 45–6, 65, 74, 81, 84–5, 89, 105, 134–7
Granville, Lord, 27
Green Papers, definition of, 169–70
Greenwood, Arthur, 39, 43
Grenville, Lord, 87
Gretton, Colonel, 95
Grey, Sir Edward, 89
Grigg, Sir E., 100

HALDANE, R. B., 29, 84, 87
Halifax, Lord, 39, 87
Hankey, Lord, 41
Harcourt, W., 19, 29, 36, 59, 77, 82, 107
Hardy, Gathorne, 82
Hartington, Lord, 36
Health, Ministry of, 36
Heath, Edward, 65, 74, 165
Henderson, Arthur, 39
Hicks-Beach, 60
Hitler, Adolf, 87
Hoare, Samuel, 39
Holland, 16
Home Affairs Committee, 41, 42, 43, 44, 119
Home Policy Committee (1942), 42
Home Rule Bill (1913), 77
Horne, Sir Robert, 39
House of Commons Disqualification Act (1957), 37
House of Commons Select Committees, 170–71
Huggins, Sir Godfrey, 85

IMPERIAL DEFENCE, COMMITTEE OF, 41, 43, 49, 89
Import Executive Committee, 42

Index

Index